Britain in fragments

Manchester University Press

Britain in fragments

Why things are falling apart

Satnam Virdee and Brendan McGeever

MANCHESTER UNIVERSITY PRESS

Published by Manchester University Press
Oxford Road, Manchester M13 9PL

www.manchesteruniversitypress.co.uk

British Library Cataloguing-in-Publication Data
A catalogue record for this book is available from the British Library

ISBN 978 1 5261 6458 2 hardback
ISBN 978 1 5261 6459 9 paperback

First published 2023

Typeset by Newgen Publishing UK

To our parents
Hardish and Surinder
and
Geraldine and Andrew
from whom we learned so much about the utopian impulse

Contents

Acknowledgements

This book is the product of a decade-long conversation about Scotland, England and the future of the British state. It began in a Glasgow pub in 2013 in the build-up to the Scottish independence referendum. The debate that night carried on over days and then weeks, and was ultimately sustained over several years. With the invaluable support of Tom Dark at Manchester University Press (MUP), we eventually committed to putting our thoughts to page. We are tremendously grateful to Tom, Laura Swift, Jen Mellor and Rebecca Parkinson at MUP, and Gail Welsh, Sarah Rendell and Jamie Hood at Newgen for the enthusiasm and commitment they have shown for the project. Also, we express particular gratitude to Ewan Gibbs and Bridget Fowler who read the entire manuscript and gave invaluable feedback on an earlier version of this book. We would also like to thank those who read draft chapters, engaged in constructive critique and provided the care that made the writing of this book possible, including Gareth Mulvey, Ashli Mullen, Maureen McBride, Smina Akhtar, Matt Dawson, Bridget Fowler, Andy Smith, Kirsteen Paton, Zoe Williams, Luke Cooper, David Featherstone, John Solomos, Michaela Benson, Imogen Tyler, Mark Rowley, David Feldman, Frank Wolf, Gleb Albert, Allan Armstrong, Ewan Gibbs, Allan Little, Aaron Winter, Nasar Meer, Ali Meghji, Scarlet Harris, Sivamohan Valluvan, Camilla Schofield, Radika Natarajan, Beverley

Skeggs, Stephen Ashe, James Renton, Jay Emery, Caroline Douglas, Geraldine Gould, Liz Douglas, David Douglas, Ian Douglas, Laura Govan, Erik Waitt, Ryan Powell, Sarah Neal, Tim Strangleman, John Narayan, Suman Gupta, Gareth Dale, Charlie Post, Mike Goldfield, Kevin Anderson and David Roediger. Early versions of our argument were presented at the Birkbeck Institute for Social Research (2015); the Havens Centre for Social Justice, University of Wisconsin (2016); the Historical Materialism conference (London, 2016 and 2017); the Berlin Wall Memorial (2017); Yale University (2017); the After Multiculturalism? conference (London, 2018); and the Westergaard Lecture, University of Sheffield (2021). A section of Chapter 3 draws on archival research carried out by Stephen Ashe as part of the Centre on Dynamics of Ethnicity (CoDE) project funded by the Economic and Social Research Council (grant number: ES/K002198/1) for which Satnam Virdee acted as Co-Investigator. Some passages of the book first appeared in articles previously published. Sections of Chapter 2 draw on Virdee's 'Socialist antisemitism and its discontents', published in *Patterns of Prejudice* 51(3–4): 356–73. Sections of Chapter 5 utilise parts of Virdee and McGeever's 'Racism, crisis, Brexit' essay, published in *Ethnic and Racial Studies* 41(10): 1802–19 and Virdee's 'Scotland and alternatives to neoliberalism', which appeared in *Soundings* 63: 55–72. Parts of the book also make use of Virdee's 'The lines of descent of the present crisis' article, published in *Sociological Review* 71: 2 (2023). We thank the respective publishers for allowing us to rework some of this material here. Finally, we acknowledge a special debt of gratitude to two dear friends and scholar-activists who are sadly no longer with us – Neil Davidson and Erik Olin Wright.

Introduction

Britain is fragmenting. The gap between the rich and poor is growing, and nobody seems able to arrest it. Politically, we have lurched to the authoritarian right amid a widening of inequalities and a diminution of hope. The malaise, which is at once political and economic, has been expressed first and foremost through a decade-long and still unfinished crisis of the British state. In 2016, Britain voted to sever its four-decade relationship with the European Union (EU). Two years earlier, in 2014, the referendum on Scottish independence came close to ending the three-century union that had been the bedrock of Britain's imperial rise to global dominance. The cracks in these once durable institutional arrangements are the most visible manifestations of the deep structural inequalities that scar the contemporary landscape. At the start of the twenty-first century, the EU and Scottish independence were remote issues in most people's lives. Today, they provide a way of talking about the grievances and injuries accrued in the neoliberal epoch. The deleterious effects of deindustrial-isation, the defeat of the labour movement and the erosion of the welfare state have all come to be expressed through the politics of nationalism. The implications of this remain as yet unknown: the British state survived Brexit, but it cannot withstand the impact of a Scottish secession. Having broken from Europe, Britain is now fragmenting from within. Will it see out the 2020s?

For many in Britain, it seems things are falling apart. At the time of writing, prices are rising, inflation is soaring and household income inequality now sits as one of the highest in Europe. The share of income going to the 1 per cent richest households has tripled from 3 per cent in the late 1970s to around 8 per cent today. Life expectancy at birth – having steadily increased between 1981 and 2010 – has stalled since 2011 and will likely decrease once excess deaths associated with austerity and the mismanagement of the COVID-19 pandemic are accounted for.[1] There has long been a geographic dimension to inequality in Britain, in par-ticular its north–south divide. What is more striking today, however, is the intensification of sub-regional inequalities, not only between cities and neighbouring small towns but within them.[2] Consider, for example, the shining behemoth of the City of London and its genteel suburban outposts intermingling with the systemic poverty of its working-class districts along with the deindustrialised towns along its south-eastern flank of north Kent. Similar patterns can be traced in Manchester, Cardiff, Glasgow and elsewhere as inequalities between the rich and labouring poor widen. And to this must be added the rising intergenerational inequality that now blights this country, with millennials born in the 1980s constituting the first post-war generation to have lower incomes during early adulthood than their parents.[3] How did it come to this?

To grasp the nature of this multi-level crisis we need to take a longer historical view. What we are witnessing today is the unravelling of the *democratic settlement*. Consisting of social welfare provisions, voting rights and an electoral vehicle representing the working class, this settlement took a century to construct and was forged between the ruling elites and the leadership of the domestic working class in Britain. From the mid-nineteenth century onwards, democracy in Britain was constructed through incremental reforms that included an ever-larger number of workers into the political process. This course of democratisation served to contain an insurgent working class, bind it to the British nation and blunt its earlier revolutionary fervour. The settlement would reach its apotheosis with the post-war welfare state. However, no sooner had the finishing touches been put in place than things began to wither on the vine amid the anti-colonial revolutions after the Second World War. As Britain lost its key financial cornerstone – empire – the basis of the democratic settlement began to crumble. A fundamental conundrum has stumped the British ruling elites ever since: how can Britain sustain its global reach and economic competitiveness while continuing to deliver the kind of social and psychic security to its working population necessary to maintain domestic social order? Both Scottish independence and Brexit are the convoluted artefacts of the failure of the British ruling class to successfully find an answer to this question.

In fact, as we show in this book, in their efforts to resolve the systemic crisis of British capitalism, successive Labour and Conservative administrations have further eroded the foundational pillars of the democratic settlement. In particular, the failure to diverge from the bipartisan commitment to neoliberalism in the aftermath of the 2007–8 financial crash effectively destroyed the post-war welfare state, producing a historic crisis of representation which has come to be filled by competing nationalist forces. This has left us, to quote Sivamohan Valluvan, in a 'nationalist moment'.[4]

Britain in Fragments offers a history of the present by tracing the labyrinthine routes through which we have arrived at this turning point. It is a book about Britain, and above all, England and Scotland. It has little to say about Wales and Northern Ireland; not because the fragmentation does not abound there – it does.[5] Rather, we place Scotland and England centre stage because it is events in these nations that are pushing Britain towards its historic point of collapse. Scotland, and more specifically, Scottish independence, is now the weak point of the British state.

At the same time, the crisis explored here is hardly one that is contained to these nations. Britain exists in a world that is on fire. Social inequalities are rising across the world as we witness a level of economic turbulence not seen since the Great Depression. Accompanying this are rising forms of social polarisation as the neoliberal consensus unravels, creating a crisis of legitimation that is global in nature. It is against this background of rupture that the political field has come to be dominated by the forces of the far right. While authoritarian politics may be back, it cannot solve the crisis. On the contrary, it will only further entrench existing divisions and inequalities. We are living through a multi-layered emergency of a capitalist world-system that is haunted by the spectre of pandemics, war and a climate catastrophe that threatens our very existence. Set against this backdrop, we hope that *Britain in Fragments* serves as a useful case study that can illuminate some of the recurring features of these consolidating social processes.

First and foremost, however, this is a book about how we arrived at this turning point in British history. What was the nature of the historic democratic settlement whose initial foundations began to be laid in Britain from the middle of the nineteenth century? Why is it unravelling before our eyes? What are the social processes that have brought us to this point? And are there social forces that can be constituted into an organised contraflow to arrest the fragmentation that so defines our precarious present? These are the questions that animate *Britain in Fragments.*

The institutional arrangements that have held Britain together are today threatening to burst asunder. Chapter 1 begins by tracing how those arrangements were incrementally put in place over the *longue durée* of the nineteenth and early twentieth centuries. It shows that Britain's convoluted journey to becoming a flawed democracy is at once a history of working-class struggle and imperial expansion. Democratisation, comprising the gradual extension of suffrage and social welfare provision, served to prevent the re-emergence of a revolutionary working-class subject that was defeated in the struggles of the 1830s and 1840s. Racism played a formative role in the making of this democratic settlement. As workers were included in ever larger numbers into the project of democracy, racism helped keep at bay any shared visions of freedom among the multitudes of the discontented. Far from being confined to liberal and conservative elites, this racist nationalism animated the labour movement as well. Those working-class men and women who took part in the building of British democracy were simultaneously extended an invitation to imagine themselves as superior to colonised subjects both at home and in the wider empire. Often, though not always, workers accepted that invitation and through their own institutional structures consolidated racialized ideas about the nation. In these ways, dominant conceptions of socialism became entangled with racist nationalism and British imperial expansion.

All too often, then, the institutions set up to advance the cause of social justice offered visions of freedom that were blunted by the stultifying force of racism. As we show, these institutions played their own formative role in the production of racialized inequalities, effectively helping to bifurcate the working class and consolidate a hierarchy within the house of labour. The emergence of the Labour Party at the start of the twentieth century exemplifies this. On the one hand a vehicle for working-class uplift, the Labour Party provided its own form of British imperial statecraft. The two power blocs in British politics therefore – Labour on the one hand, and the Conservative and Liberal elites on the other – held a shared commitment to empire and nationalism that stunted the full realisation of democracy. This tragic entwining of imperialism and class struggle set the parameters for the century to come; only in episodic moments, discussed in this book, would workers in their multi-ethnicity find ways to prise open a vision of class that broke free from the trappings of race and nation, and point instead towards an expansive and inclusive future for all. Ultimately, *Britain in Fragments* is written in the hope that the modern working class and its allies may be able to rediscover that emancipatory impulse.

At the same time, the book explains why the odds remain so heavily stacked against the cause of labour.

Chapter 2 follows this history through to the post-war era and the consolidation of the welfare state – the culmination of the democratic settlement. Seen by many as the golden age of social democracy, we present a different reading, suggesting there was nothing romantic about this coveted period in British history. Undoubtedly, this was a significant moment of working-class advancement, reform and democratisation. But it was also accompanied by a carnival of racist reaction from all social classes, bringing misery to Asian and Caribbean lives and tarnishing their hopes and dreams of a better life in Britain. Racism was central to this welfare settlement in two senses. First, imperial plunder continued to provide the material resources for this historic process of working-class upliftment. Second, the post-war inter-class truce was secured, in part, through the super-exploitation of migrant labour from the Indian sub-continent and Caribbean, a process that reinforced the relatively privileged position of parts of the white British working class. Just as the National Health Service was constituted and full employment declared, colour bars were erected across British industries. Racism, then, would prove to be the Achilles heel of the project of working-class democratisation. Finally, just as the finishing touches were being put in place to this flawed democratic settlement, its foundations began to crack amid the anti-colonial revolutions across the empire. Chapter 2 traces these developments during the years 1945 to 1970, as the British state struggled to forge new strategies to maintain social order and capitalist rule.

Those efforts ran to ground during the turbulence of the 1970s and early 1980s, as relative British economic decline mutated into a full-blown capitalist crisis. This period saw open class conflict between the state, employers and the organised labour movement. Chapter 3 charts how, amid this turbulence, new utopian socialist projects burst into the open, moving well beyond the familiar repertoires of Labourism, mobilising the oppressed in all its multitude. Between a welfare settlement in crisis and a neoliberal Conservative Party whose victory was not yet assured, history and hope seemed to chime as the long-standing collective action against racism waged by Caribbean and Asian workers helped stretch the labour movement to encompass the working class in all its ethnic diversity. Increasingly, working-class struggles became entangled in new anti-racist cultures that hinted at a different way of living.

Tragically, these fragile visions of an optimistic future were crushed by the capitalist counter-revolution known as Thatcherism. Margaret Thatcher's General Election victory in 1979 would launch the most concerted attack on the organised working class since the 1920s, heralding the rise of neoliberalism. Accompanying its repressive measures were new forms of cultural racism that re-divided the working class into racialized camps. This chapter shows how the transition to the neoliberal epoch was never inevitable. Rather, it required the extinguishing of hope, the crushing of an emergent multi-ethnic class subject.

The 1980s, then, mark a key moment in our still-unfolding journey towards de-democratisation and the reversal of the settlement that had held firm for a century. The empire, which provided the economic basis for domestic social stability, was gone. And the welfare settlement was thrown into reverse, as capital reasserted itself over labour. In this historic moment, the working class was effectively denied the right to express its collective voice in the neoliberal institutional arrangements of the British state. The different foundational pillars that secured the terms of the democratic settlement were beginning to unravel at pace. This historical backdrop of reversal and working-class defeat, we suggest, provides the way to make sense of the national fragmentations that define British politics today. In the vacuum created by the hollowing-out of working-class and socialist cultures of resistance, new modes of belonging and stigmatisation were inserted into everyday political life.

This is the theme addressed in Chapter 4. If Thatcher defeated the working class, New Labour erased it. Following its defeat at the 1992 General Election, Labour was faced with a historic question: would it accept the principles of neo-liberal capitalism already consolidated by more than a decade of Conservative rule? Or would it retain its stated mission of working-class uplift? These questions were posed in a radically transformed context, one in which the working class was now a defeated class – a social force shorn of its collective power following the assault of Thatcherism. This moment was seized by the thinkers and modernisers of what would become known as New Labour. Building from a premise that the party was too dependent on the trade unions and too oriented to the working class, Labour was remade to reflect the 'realities' of Thatcherism. Driven intellectually by key figures such as Tony Blair and Gordon Brown, New Labour's modernisers now went in search of a different constituency, defined as 'aspirational, hard-working families' and 'middle England'. This shift in politics and in philosophy would see Labour assent to the main principles of global capitalism, crafting a form of social neoliberalism that accepted key features of Thatcherism while conjoining them to a programme of increased public spending in essential infrastructure.

Having erased the old language of class from its repertoire and political worldview, New Labour crafted new categories of belonging that remade class through the idea of race. In particular, different fractions of the working class were organised into ethno-racialized appellations through Labour's discourse of state multiculturalism. In the absence of an organised and multi-ethnic working-class subject, racialized identifications such as the 'white working class' came to fill the political vacuum both as a force for mobilisation and recognition. This racialization of class combined with imperialist wars in Iraq and Afghanistan produced powerful new racisms, including, most notably, anti-Muslim racism. The effect was to energise claims that 'Muslim culture' was in some way incompatible with modern liberal democratic states like Britain and their intrinsic commitment to so-called tolerance and diversity. These developments helped pave the way for the racist blowback of Brexit in the decade that followed.

The undoing of the democratic settlement reached its culmination amid the Great Recession of 2007–8, which is the subject of Chapter 5. When New Labour committed itself to austerity as a way of resolving the crisis, something historic took place: one of the crumbling pillars that had wedded the working class to the British idea was finally kicked away. This effective merger of the two main parties consolidated a break in the representational politics of class and party. Any sense that the Labour Party was a vehicle for working-class advancement was lost in this moment. Austerity – and the failure of Labour to challenge it – buried that idea. New Labour's accommodation to neoliberalism and its capitulation to austerity would ensure the party would spend successive terms out of office.

But the consequences of this rupture between party and class extended well beyond the narrow question of Labour's fortunes. It produced a historic loss of authority, a crisis of representation not just for Labour, but for the British state and its institutions. In Scotland, support for Labour would fall away, precipitating the dramatic rise of the Scottish National Party (SNP) on a centre-left terrain; in England, meanwhile, the collapse of Labourism was to be accompanied by the rise of an authoritarian racist backlash. The unravelling of British democracy, then, has produced nationalist secessionist movements in Brexit and in Scottish independence that threaten the very integrity of the British state.

Even the Conservative Party – a foundational pillar of that state and its democratic settlement – has not been immune to such instability. The comprehensive Tory victory at the 2019 General Election was predicated on the party's ability to bring together the contradictory forces that drove the Brexit vote three years earlier. However, the subsequent resignations of both Boris Johnson and Liz Truss indicate that these currents may be fundamentally irreconcilable. The Conservative Party is showing signs of fragmentation between two blocs, one which favours a deregulated Singapore on the Thames, and another committed to public investment to 'level-up' the country. As these tensions burst into the open, the Tories may yet find themselves hoisted on a petard of their own making.

As the arrangements crafted over the last century are thrown into reverse, Britain is revealed as a society in fragments. Can a political force be awakened today which can arrest the fragmentation and conjure visions of equality and freedom for all? This book concludes by going in search of one.

Notes

1   Robert Joyce and Xiaowei Xu, 'Inequalities in the Twenty-First Century: Introducing the IFS Deaton Review' (The Institute for Fiscal Studies, 2019), https://ifs.org.uk/inequality/chapter/brief ing-note/.

2   Polina Obolenskaya and John Hills, 'Flat-Lining or Seething beneath the Surface? Two Decades of Changing Economic Inequality in the UK', *Oxford Review of Economic Policy* 35, no. 3 (2019): 467–89; Susan Watkins, 'Britain's Decade of Crisis', *New Left Review* 1, no. 121 (2020): 7.

3   Joyce and Xu, 'Inequalities in the Twenty-First Century', 11.

4   Sivamohan Valluvan, *The Clamour of Nationalism: Race and Nation in Twenty-First-Century Britain* (Manchester: Manchester University Press, 2019).

5   On race, class and nation in Ireland and Wales, see Chris Gilligan, *Northern Ireland and the Crisis of Anti-Racism: Rethinking Racism and Sectarianism* (Manchester: Manchester University Press, 2017); Chris Gilligan, 'Methodological Nationalism and the Northern Ireland Blind-Spot in Ethnic and Racial Studies', *Ethnic and Racial Studies* (3 August 2021): 1–21, DOI: 10.1080/ 01419870.2021.1950793; Robbie McVeigh, 'Living the Peace Process in Reverse: Racist Violence and British Nationalism in Northern Ireland', *Race & Class* 56, no. 4 (2015): 3–25; Robin Mann and Steve Fenton, *Nation, Class and Resentment: The Politics of National Identity in England, Scotland and Wales* (Basingstoke: Palgrave Macmillan, 2017).

1   A flawed democracy

We can begin to understand the current crisis of legitimation in Britain by taking a historical view. The institutional arrangements that are threatening to burst asunder today were incrementally put in place through the nineteenth and twentieth centuries. What are the most important features of this democratic settlement? What were the competing social forces that helped construct it? And how was this settlement able to secure the trust of the majority of the population within the internal boundaries of Britain? Grasping the answers to these questions will enable us to understand why things are unravelling now.

It is often remarked that England is home to the mother of all parliaments. Yet its successor states, Britain and the United Kingdom, only belatedly moved towards democratising the polity during the mid-nineteenth century with the granting of trade union rights and voting rights to a minority of the skilled male working class.[1] Until 1867, the British Parliament – elected on a restricted property-based franchise – was a debating chamber for determining policy in the general interest of capital.[2]

Britain's journey towards democracy was the product of a convoluted set of interactions between the emergence of the working class as a social force and the desire of political elites to maintain social order to ensure the uninterrupted accumulation of capital and expand its geopolitical reach through imperialism. Having defeated an insurgent proletariat in the 1840s, the dominant ruling bloc of Conservative and Liberal imperial nationalists incorporated a layer of skilled working men into the sphere of democratic politics as a way of preventing the re-emergence of a cohesive, revolutionary working class. A racializing nationalism along with the economic returns from empire were central to this containment strategy, with their inclusion secured in opposition to colonised subjects both at home and abroad.

While Liberal and Conservative imperial elites established this route to prevent the re-emergence of an insurgent proletariat, another bloc consolidated it further: the Labour Party. Over the course of the twentieth century, Labour situated its demands for working-class inclusion on the same ideological terrain of nationalism. The labour movement's conception of national belonging was certainly more expansive than that of the imperial bloc: it sought greater rights and welfare for those excluded from the democratic process. Nevertheless, it insisted on legitimating its demands in opposition to the most recent wave of migrants. This shared commitment to racialized nationalism and empire was a constitutive feature of the politics of both ruling blocs that helped secure voting rights and social welfare for the working class between the 1850s and 1940s.

Democratisation against democracy

A regime is democratic in so far as

> it maintains broad citizenship, binding consultation of citizens at large with respect to governmental activities and personnel, as well as protection of citizens from arbitrary action by governmental agents. Citizenship consists, in this context, of mutual rights and obligations binding governmental agents to whole categories of people who are subject to the government's authority.[3]

British ruling elites had long regarded their domestic non-elite population with as much disdain as their so-called imperial subjects, that is, as an inherently difficult and disposable population. Typical of such opinion was the leading statesman and philosopher Francis Bacon. Just prior to the first departure of English ships to Virginia in 1606, Bacon wrote to James I making the case for colonisation on the grounds that sending the English poor abroad would gain 'a double commodity, in the avoidance of [such] people here, and in making use of them there'.[4] Similarly, when the economic returns from violent extraction and expropriation in the colonies contributed to securing Britain's transition to industrial capitalism,[5] there was initially widespread elite indifference to the devastation of living conditions it wreaked on the former peasant and artisan. Already dispossessed through enclosure and stigmatised as vagrants and vagabonds as they searched for new forms of work, members of these so-called lower classes were pulled from the countryside to work in the engine-room of industrial capitalism – the 'dark satanic mills', as William Blake so aptly described them. Here, they found themselves 'more exploited, more insecure and more miserable than before'.[6]

Ruthless exploitation, including of working-class children, was a constitutive feature of this new industrial capitalism. The industrialist and social reformer, John Fielden, carefully observing the establishment of large cotton factories in the counties of Derbyshire, Lancashire and Nottinghamshire, argued that a new era of child enslavement had been inaugurated in Britain:

> The custom was for the master to clothe his apprentices and to feed and lodge them in an 'apprentice house' near the factory; overseers were appointed to see to the works, whose interest it was to work the children to the utmost, because their pay was in proportion to the quantity of work that they could exact. Cruelty was, of course, the consequence ... In many of the manufacturing districts, but particularly ... Lancashire,

cruelties of the most heart-rending kind were practised upon
the unoffending and friendless creatures who were thus
consigned to the charge of master-manufacturers; they were
harassed to the brink of death by excess of labour ... flogged,
fettered and tortured in the most exquisite refinement of
cruelty ... they were in many cases starved to the bone while
flogged to their work and ... even in some instances ... were
driven to commit suicide.[7]

By drawing attention to this passage our aim is not to
construct an equivalence between the barbaric practices
associated with colonial conquest and those associated with
capitalist exploitation domestically. Rather, it is to illuminate
their imbrication and connectedness in an emergent transnational capitalism so that we may recognise more clearly the
wilful indifference the British elites showed to the suffering
of all subjugated populations within its ever-expanding territorial jurisdiction.

And it was precisely such wilful indifference that helped
produce an insurgent working class and a sustained cycle of
economic and political resistance to save long-established
ways of life in the first half of the nineteenth century.[8] Parts
of this working class understood with great clarity how its
interests were opposed directly to those of the capitalist
class and the political system known as Old Corruption.[9]
For more than half a century, they refused to bend to the
will of capitalist discipline, establishing a powerful organisational infrastructure ranging from combination societies
in the workplace to the political movement Chartism. They
invented innovative practices from the strike to the mass petition that served as transmission belts of political radicalism
into the wider working class, helping to establish visions of
a society differently organised in which all men – but only
occasionally women – might play a full part.[10]

Significantly, this working class was a multi-ethnic formation from the moment of its inception. The demand for labour
was such that 750,000 migrants from the colony of Ireland

were pulled across the Irish Sea by 1847. And from further afield came a smaller population of people of African descent, including former slaves from the United States and the Caribbean.[11] Further, the Industrial Revolution had coincided with revolutions in France in 1789 and Haiti in 1791. The latter illuminated how it was the self-activity of people of African descent that forced the revolutionary regime in France into issuing a decree abolishing slavery premised on the 'aristocracy of the skin',[12] thereby ensuring the promise of 'liberty, equality and fraternity' was extended to everyone. The corresponding societies, established in Britain in the wake of these revolutions, forged 'a new democratic consciousness'[13] by drawing together advocates of multiple radical causes, including Irish independence, opposition to the aristocracy and to slavery, and an extension of rights and freedoms for working people. Their objective was nothing less than to transform 'the mob' 'by education and agitation' from 'followers of the camp' to followers of 'the standard of liberty'.[14]

The imperial British state now found itself confronted with the most pressing of dilemmas, namely, how best to contain this insurgent multi-ethnic working class that threatened to disrupt the social order and the accumulation of capital. Racialized outsiders of Irish Catholic and African descent played a formative role in universalising this wave of class struggle in the first half of the nineteenth century. Drawing on the radical ideas of the French Revolution they prised open a Pandora's box, stimulating an array of democratic demands which were incompatible with the interests of the rising forces of industrial capitalism.[15] Tragically, and despite the successive waves of innovative collective action informed by 'an indomitable and generous spirit', this first industrial working class of world history would eventually go on to experience a crushing defeat at the hands of 'established authority'.[16]

The repressive apparatuses of the state were decisive in securing this catastrophic defeat with workers jailed, deported to the colonies and their organisations outlawed. But repression was not the state's only weapon. The 1830s and 1840s also marked the beginnings of the sustained deployment of state racism to differentiate and divide the multi-ethnic working class within Britain – a racism that remains with us to this day. One of its key features was its disparaging portrayal of Chartism – the movement for universal male suffrage – as foreign, alien and an inauthentic expression of the desires and wishes of the British worker. In the popular press, it was claimed that the English working class had been misled by Irish Catholics and Africans to undertake forms of collective action that were incompatible with the British character.[17] At the trial of one of the leaders of London Chartism – William Cuffay – *The Times* newspaper referred to the social movement as the 'black man and his party'. It went onto describe Cuffay as 'half a "nigger"'. Some of the others are Irishmen. We doubt if there are half-a-dozen Englishmen in the whole lot.'[18] Elsewhere, it reported on how appalled it was by 'that extravagance of wild sedition which, for want of any other adjective, must be denominated "Irish"', and how London was endangered by 'the Irish love of knife, dagger and poison bowl'.[19] Meanwhile, the satirical magazine *Punch* regularly referred to the Chartist leaders of 1848 as 'MOONEY, ROONEY, HOOLAN, DOOLAN'.[20]

The defeat of this insurgent working-class subject proved catastrophic, resulting in a 'profound caesura' in British working-class history.[21] The class that was forged by the currents of Jacobinism and Owenite socialism now retreated into a state of 'prolonged catatonic withdrawal. The most insurgent working class in Europe became the most numbed and docile.'[22] Accompanying the disappearance of its combativity was the almost total collapse of its radical political consciousness, leading one historian to observe how the entire body of socialists 'might all have been comfortably got into one smallish hall'.[23] The passing of this 'heroic age of the proletariat' gave the mid-Victorian elites the necessary breathing space to deliberate possible mechanisms that would discourage any future re-emergence of the working class as an autonomous, insurgent social force in British politics and so prevent what they feared most – the 'exclusive rule of a single class'.[24] A number of more politically moderate organisations such as the Universal League for the Material Elevation of the Industrious Classes and the Reform League emerged during the 1860s. They sought to uplift parts of the working class through the re-acquisition of the right to assembly and the reform of the Master and Servant Act. But it would be the demand for voting rights that would come to dominate political discussion.

The proposal to extend the franchise to parts of the working class opened up a fissure within the two ruling political parties – Liberal and Conservative. On the one hand, the majority of Conservatives along with a minority of Liberals remained highly sceptical about enfranchising the working class. Typical of this standpoint was Robert Lowe, Liberal MP for Calne, who asked, 'If you want venality, if you want ignorance, if you want drunkenness, and facility for being intimidated; or if … you want impulsive, unreflecting, and violent people, where do you look for them in the constituencies? Do you go to the top or to the bottom?'[25] On the other hand, the majority of Liberals and a minority of Conservatives were increasingly swayed by the arguments of William Gladstone, who argued that enfranchising a small part of the working class would ensure 'you will never have one class combining against other classes'.[26] Liberal figures like Gladstone along with the Conservative Disraeli were astute enough to understand the working class of mid-Victorian Britain was no longer the insurgent political force it once was, but one that had been 'divided into a politically moderate aristocracy of labour, ready to accept capitalism, and a politically ineffective, because unorganised and leaderless, proletarian plebs, which presented no major danger'.[27]

Such an impression was no doubt consolidated by the growing power and influence of the politically moderate leaders of the new model unionism. Men like George Odjer, Henry Broadhurst and Robert Applegarth co-operated with parts of the Liberal Party in organisations such as the Reform

League in their quest to extend suffrage to the skilled working man. Gladstone, in particular, 'frequently contrasted the harmony of the 1860s with the class antagonisms of his youth'.[28] Such co-operation across the class divide helped open the eyes of some of the elites to other ways of ruling that relied less on coercion and more on the manufacture of consent. An increasing emphasis came to be placed on representational distinctions and gradations within the working class. A conception of the labouring poor 'fused into a homogenous mass of the discontented and oppressed'[29] was replaced by discourses which separated 'the workers' from 'the poor'. What emerged were 'respectable' and 'unrespectable' parts of the working class, with respectability denoting the penetration of middle-class values such as sobriety, sacrifice and a settled domestic life.

Reginald Horsman reminds us that the middle of the nineteenth century was also the moment when 'the importance of race, of "blood", was assumed in a manner quite unlike that of one hundred years before'.[30] As a consequence, class-based distinctions were also wilfully entangled with elite racism, both in opposition to imperial subjects abroad[31] and those outsiders settled within Britain itself.[32] The long association of British national belonging with Protestantism[33] was strengthened by the racializing signifier 'Anglo-Saxon'. Those communities of Irish Catholic descent settled in Britain now found themselves doubly excluded from the imagined national community, not only as Catholics but as members of a so-called inferior race of Celts.[34] Visually, a persistent caricature of the Irish working man and woman developed in mid-Victorian Britain which 'emphasise[d] the prognathous features of the Irish labouring class: a bulge in the lower part of the face, the chin prominent, the mouth big, the forehead receding, a short nose, often upturned and with yawning nostrils: the simianising of the Irish'.[35] And accompanying the generation of the racialized categories Anglo-Saxon and Irish Celt were a series of immutable cultural differences with the former imputed as masculine, freedom loving and capable of self-government and the latter represented as feminine, childish, addicted to violence and authoritarian control.[36]

Similarly, the colonies provided a benchmark allowing the British 'to determine what they did not want to be and who they thought they were'.[37] Both Liberals and radicals complained about the 'inconsistency of refusing to our fellow – subjects at home – rights which we freely confer upon them in the colonies'.[38] These individuals were of course referring to those enfranchised populations of British descent resident in Australia, New Zealand and elsewhere throughout the British empire and not the conquered non-European and indigenous populations. In fact, these sorts of racialized distinctions were consolidated by events such as the Morant Bay rebellion in Jamaica in 1865,[39] when even liberal opinion ruled that black men and women were unfit for self-government. Lord Grey, Secretary of State for the Colonies and a lifetime supporter of emancipation, proclaimed that 'From all the evidence I have been able to collect, I have come to the conclusion that for many years to come the negroes will be unfit to exercise political power.'[40] It was in distinction to Irish Catholics at home and non-Europeans abroad that a virtuous, racialized transnational Anglo-Saxon Protestant male subject with ancestral origins in Britain was birthed.

The Liberal leader, Gladstone, did his utmost to reassure the still large constituency of ruling class sceptics, including those within his own party, that skilled working men 'are our fellow-subjects, our fellow-Christians, our own flesh and blood'.[41] The crucial issue was 'to understand the lines we draw' and include 'the most intelligent' and 'the most independent',[42] while other advocates claimed such men would not threaten the national culture, would not 'make us any less English, or less national than we are now'.[43] All the time, such proposals for racialized national inclusion into the polity remained deeply structured by classist ideologies, suggesting this newly enfranchised working-class constituency would not be recognised as equal citizens. Gladstone, for example, insisted on making his case for extending the franchise partly on the grounds that skilled working men should be given the opportunity to demonstrate 'their allegiance to their betters'.

Justifying his enactment of the 1867 Reform Act, the Conservative Benjamin Disraeli patiently reassured those remaining sceptics in his party that 'I think England is safe in the race of men who inhabit her; that she is safe in something much more precious than her accumulated capital – her accumulated experience; she is safe in her national character, in her fame, in the tradition of a thousand years, and in that glorious future which I believe awaits her.'[44] His use of the idea of race was not coincidental. Throughout this period, he was unswervingly insistent that 'race' was the key to history: 'Progress and reaction ... are but words to mystify the millions. They mean nothing, they are nothing, they are phrases and not facts. All is race. In the structure, the decay, and the development of the various families of man, the vicissitudes of history will find their main solution.'[45]

In advocating for the enfranchisement of the so-called skilled Anglo-Saxon working man, figures like Gladstone and Disraeli were driven by a highly instrumentalised desire to contain the industrial working class and thereby prevent it from re-emerging as an autonomous and insurgent social force in British political life. The intention was not to democratise the system but widen the social base of elite class rule by incorporating the moderate and deferential worker and so prevent the creation of a mass democracy informed by the principle of one person, one vote, one value. As Disraeli, the architect of the 1867 Reform Act, put it: 'We do not, however, live – and I trust it will never be the fate of this country to live – under a democracy.'[46]

While this clarifies the motivation of elites in democratising the internal polity of the imperial British state, we must still ask why such measures proved so successful in drawing this skilled stratum of working-class men into the domain of democratic politics under the hegemony of the ruling elite. Part of the answer is provided in a series of influential essays penned by Perry Anderson and Tom Nairn in which they claim the English (although not British) working class was born premature in so far as its arrival on the stage of history preceded the emergence of socialism.[47] Having no access to a progressive ideology that might have shaped their opposition to industrial capitalism and potentially open them up to its radical transformation, the English working class instead 'remained for generations attached to pre-industrial traditions, their resistance to capitalism … also a reaching back towards this way of life [such that] radicalism was in essence the restoration of a kind of English golden age'.[48]

Nairn and Anderson perhaps underestimate how easily ideas could travel across nationalised borders to inform a progressive democratic consciousness amid the peak of the working-class insurgency in the early nineteenth century.[49] Nevertheless, they are correct that the dominant tendency was for the working class of Britain to legitimise their struggles for economic and social justice with reference to a mythical past. As a result, elite discourses about racialized Anglo-Saxons increasingly chimed with the oral traditions of the working class that referenced the 'ancient liberties and rights of free-born Englishmen'. This is why these understandings of immutable racialized difference introduced by the elites consolidated themselves within the cultural and political life of the working class. And for the respectable Anglo-Saxon working man, the advantages of embracing a racializing imperial nationalism were unprecedented and effectively heralded the era of democratic citizenship encompassing not only the acquisition of the franchise but wider social reform.

The social ties between the skilled working man and the Liberal Party in particular were strengthened further over the course of the 1870s with the recently established Trades Union Congress (TUC) lobbying successfully for the legalisation of trade unions (1871 Trade Union Act). And both

Liberal and Conservative governments accompanied such legislation in the workplace with social reforms aimed at improving the wellbeing of the working class, including the 1872 Public Health Act, the 1875 Artisans' Dwelling Act and the 1870 and 1880 Education Acts – the latter making school compulsory for children under eleven.

These reforms encouraged a belief among this constituency of skilled working men (and eventually their families) that they too held a stake in the British nation. After all, this sense of national identification was now undergirded by a modest yet unprecedented degree of political entitlement and economic security. There were now formal institutional arrangements in place which enabled and facilitated the advocacy of working-class interests. Their interests as craft workers and engineers could now be understood as entirely compatible with active membership of the nation such that the language and politics of class became nationalised. And they also now acquired within their arsenal the option of wilfully deploying the advantage of laying claim to membership of the ruling race of the nation. This tactic was deployed with increasing regularity to exclude Irish Catholics and other racialized minority workers from the more skilled jobs on the grounds that they were not 'racially British'.[50]

Of central importance to the success of such racism was the extent to which it could secure the acquiescence of parts of the subaltern class. In symbolically and materially revaluing some parts of the population while simultaneously devaluing others, elite deployment of racism aimed at engineering a chasm within the working class. The consequences were devastating: those who were revalued became indifferent to, even complicit in, the suffering and degradation of those populations marked as 'racially inferior', including within the same territorial space.

These subtle changes in political consciousness explain why this enfranchised stratum of the working class would reciprocate by voting loyally for their benefactors – the

Liberal Party of Gladstone. It would ensure the Liberals remained in power throughout much of this period of British domination of the capitalist world-system. A historic class compromise had been reached by the third quarter of the nineteenth century marking the successful integration of a minority of the domestic male working class into an elite-led imperial British nationalism.[51]

The significance of empire to this partial democratisation of British society lay not only in the regimes of racialized representation that were deployed to determine the type of working man who would be enfranchised, but also in the economic returns from colonial conquest. By the mid-nineteenth century, Britain's domination of the world market through empire (both formal and informal) and its enforcement of international free trade in the era of diplomatic-industrial imperialism had transformed it into the hegemon of the capitalist world-economy. As a result, this opening moment of democratisation occurred when the apparatuses of the state were confident that they were rich enough to be able to afford such changes.[52] In this sense, Britain's ruling class established 'legitimacy and quiescence through imperial revenue'.[53] The political class had finally discovered a process of ruling in a more consensual manner at home, one that was in keeping with the maintenance of social order, the accumulation of capital and imperial conquest.

The new unionism and socialist nationalism

While a historic class compromise had been cemented, even after the Liberal Party's belated enactment of the Third Reform Act in 1884, the majority of Britain's domestic population (all adult women and around 40 per cent of adult working men) remained unenfranchised. In fact, 'there was little that was democratic about the Third Reform Act ... the vote was still widely seen as a privilege bestowed on the deserving and respectable'.[54] In essence, the dominant power of the established landed gentry and capitalist elites remained largely uncontested. They could also now lay claim to the added legitimacy and trust conferred on them by the complicity and political manoeuvrings of the trade union leadership of the skilled male working class. However, class compromises, while durable, were not permanent and could become unsettled, particularly during periods of sustained multi-level crisis. By the mid-1870s, Britain had begun to lose its manufacturing advantage to France, Germany and the United States with its leadership of the capitalist world-system increasingly under threat. The Long Depression that followed comprised a series of economic slumps in 1875, 1880 and 1884, producing persistently high levels of unemployment. It was amid these deteriorating economic circumstances that the beginnings of a further moment of democratisation can be discerned.

It initially found expression in a wave of industrial unrest referred to as the new unionism. In Scotland, it began as early as 1880 with the rebellion of the Highland crofters, urban industrial workers and miners working in the coalfields of Lanarkshire.[55] In England it was initiated by the large demonstrations against unemployment in 1886 and 1887, the strike by young women and girls at the Bryant & May match factory in Bow in 1888, and culminated in the great dock strike of 1889. This was the revolt of the so-called residuum, a rebellion of the 'lowest of the low' in the hierarchy of labour comprising the 'unrespectable' and the labouring poor. These groups of workers helped expand the trade union movement beyond its traditional preserve of skilled craft workers such that within a year of the dock strike, more than 350,000 unskilled workers had been organised. By 1892, overall union membership had doubled from 750,000 in 1888 to 1,576,000 in 1892, transforming the nature of trade unionism in Britain.[56]

Central to the success of this movement was the ideology of socialism, with men and women in the Scottish Labour Party, the Social Democratic Federation (SDF), the Socialist League and later the Independent Labour Party (ILP) playing a formative role. Some of the key figures included John Dunn, William

Nairn, James Connolly, Bruce Glasier, Eleanor Marx, Annie Besant, William Morris, Will Thorne, Ben Tillett, Keir Hardie, John Burns and Tom Mann. A veritable cornucopia of socialist thought and practice informed such collective action in its formative stages. It ranged from the revolutionary internationalism of William Morris and Eleanor Marx's Socialist League to the Irish republican culture of many of the striking matchgirls, dockers and gas workers to the entangled politics of class and Scottish nationalism of the activists from the Scottish Labour Party. However, the majority of activists who shaped the political trajectory of the new unionism adhered to a more limited understanding of socialism. In its dominant religious form, such socialism saw the struggle as 'one of good versus evil, of fairness and decency against rapaciousness and exploitation. The object was to "bring down a little more heaven to earth".'[57] Such a philosophy was inspired less by *Capital* and more by the Bible, or, as Keir Hardie put it, '[I learnt my] Socialism in the New Testament'.[58] This perspective didn't require overthrowing the existing capitalist state but taking charge of it to make it 'easy to do right and difficult to do wrong'.[59] And it would find institutional expression in the ILP when it was established in 1893.

Many of these activists married their belief in socialism with an almost unthinking attachment to nationalism – sometimes of the British variant but more often an English, Scottish or even Irish republican type. Unlike the racialized imperial nationalism of the Liberal and Conservative elites, however, these forms of socialist nationalism had an inherently democratising impulse. They aimed at expanding the active citizenry so that it encompassed the large majority of the domestic working class who not only remained unenfranchised but continued to suffer great social and material deprivation. A political route to secure social justice had been manufactured by the Liberal and Conservative imperial elites. It allowed a small layer of working men to be included in the nation as a means of preventing the re-emergence of the working class as an autonomous force in politics. But these socialist activists prised it open further by situating their demands for those still excluded as being for class *and* country.

As Henry Hyndman, the leader of the secular SDF, put it, 'A great democratic English Republic has ever been the dream of the noblest of our race ... to bring about such a Republic is the cause for which we Socialists agitate today.'[60] A central feature of the new unionism was the re-emergence of a multi-ethnic class solidarity. In the urban conurbations of Scotland, Irish Catholic migrants conjoined with Gaelic Highlanders and Protestant Scots to battle poverty and unemployment while England saw a coming together of workers of English as well as Irish Catholic descent. In part, this inclusive approach of the socialist leaders was a recognition of the formative role that Irish activists like Ben Tillett, Will Thorne, James Larkin and James Sexton played in catalysing such working-class action across Britain.[61] The Labour Party politician Morgan Phillips once observed that the party 'owes more to Methodism than to Marxism'. In cities like Glasgow, Liverpool, London and Manchester it owed as much to a form of social Catholicism.[62]

Antisemitism: the underside of socialist nationalism

These socialist ideas of class-based national belonging were undoubtedly more expansive than those of the elite-led project of imperial nationalism. Unlike the latter, they encompassed, as we have seen, the so-called residuum, Gaelic Highlanders, as well as those of Irish Catholic descent. However, they remained incapable of including the most recent migrants and refugees: above all, Jews from Eastern Europe. Many of these same socialist leaders helped shape and give coherence to antisemitism such that older religiously inflected antisemitic representations of Jews as 'Christ-killers' and 'usurers' were incrementally and unevenly overlain by an emergent set of representations that came to associate the Jewish worker with the economic and social degradation of the English working class. Ben Tillett, a socialist leader who was instrumental in forging solidarity between English and Irish Catholic dockworkers in the East End of London, could not extend the hand of friendship to the newly arrived East European Jews. Instead, he claimed '[t]he influx of continental pauperism aggravates and multiplies the number of ills which press so heavily on us ... Foreigners come to London in large numbers, herd together in habitations unfit for beasts, the sweating system allowing the more grasping and shrewd a life of comparative ease in superintending their work.'[63]

The historian Eric Hobsbawm once described the new unionism as a 'recrudescence of revolutionary utopianism'[64] that 'challenged the very foundations of the capitalist system'.[65] We see it differently. Throughout the new unionism, socialist nationalist support for Jewish workers remained lukewarm at best, and was shaped by a pragmatic, instrumental collectivism that recognised the need to curtail expressions of antisemitism only because it risked fatally undermining the broader class solidarity forged in opposition to the employers. In this sense, their solidarity with the migrant Jew was strategic, not principled, and was primarily born of a rational calculation of the costs and benefits of multi-ethnic solidarity. Typical of such a standpoint was the aforementioned Ben Tillett, who, when referring to the Jewish workers taking collective action, declared: 'yes, you are our brothers, and we will stand by you. But we wish you had not come.'[66]

In this brand of socialist antisemitism, Jewish workers were understood not only as a super-exploited fraction of the working class, but an alien body, antithetical to British workers' interests and responsible for undermining their conditions of living. This image of the Jew as an anti-working-class figure was reinforced when it came to entwine with another set of stereotypes of the Jew as the quintessential embodiment of capitalism. This trope, consistently drawn on by Henry Hyndman – founder and leader of the SDF – saw the capitalist Jew in almost demonic terms, lying at the centre of 'a sinister "gold international" destined one day to be locked in mortal conflict with the "red international" of socialism'.[67] Taken together, these socialist visions trapped Jews in a double-bind as capitalist parasite and sweated labour opposed to working-class interests and the socialist nationalist project of democratic change. And it would eventually lead to increasingly shrill calls for immigration control which culminated in the introduction of the Aliens Act of 1905.[68]

The Labour Party: connecting working-class justice to British imperialism

Regardless of the blind spot of racist antisemitism, elements of the state and employing class were sufficiently perturbed by the rise of socialism and the new unionism's demands for democratisation that they set about undermining the legal position of trade unionism, particularly the right to picket. By the late 1890s, the employers had clawed back many of the gains made by the multi-ethnic labouring poor, reducing their unions to around 150,000 members.[69] Unable to secure their objectives through industrial action alone, socialist activists increasingly turned to securing a parliamentary voice for its working-class constituency. The ILP – a Christian socialist formation and very much the authentic voice of working-class activists – would field 29 candidates at the 1895 General Election. However, it failed abysmally, garnering a paltry 44,325 votes. When Keir Hardie failed to win a parliamentary seat in 1896, the disappointed ILP leadership concluded that the prospects for socialism were more remote than they had imagined.[70] The time for making socialists was over.

The reversal of the organisational gains and the electoral failure of the ILP produced a more pragmatic working-class politics as the twentieth century dawned. It forced the ILP's leadership to forge alliances and electoral pacts with sympathisers of the 'working-class cause', including Liberal-leaning trade union leaders and the middle-class reformers of the Fabian Society. In 1900, these different components came together in the Labour Representation Committee (LRC), and by 1906, the LRC had become the Labour Party, with the ILP providing much of its activist base.[71] The intention of the ILP leaders was to establish a party of labour (no longer socialist) that was electorally viable. By challenging the Liberals and Conservatives for state power, the objective was to secure the inclusion of the previously unrespectable working class into the national polity as equal and active citizens. But this would also bring in its wake additional political commitments.

Unlike the ILP leadership of Hardie, Glasier and Macdonald, who were opposed to imperialism, the Fabians were strong advocates of the British empire. Acutely aware of elite anxieties about Britain's capacity to fulfil its imperial mission since the Boer War, figures like Sidney and Beatrice Webb, Graham Wallas and George Bernard Shaw now seized the opportunity to reinterpret the ILP objective of economic and social justice for the working class as not an end in itself, but rather as a means to maintain Britain's imperialist ambitions abroad.[72] A corollary of the welding of the cause of working-class upliftment to the project of empire were the efforts to make workers more conscious of 'their' empire and particularly the role they needed to play in its defence.[73] In these years, Sidney Webb publicly commended Lord Roseberry for his imperial outlook, while George Bernard Shaw, in *Fabianism and the Empire*, justified the British conquest of the Transvaal, and the opening up of China to European capitalism, on the grounds that 'states with a higher civilisation had a right to take over backward states'.[74]

The racializing logic of social imperialism began to permeate even those political structures of the working class which had been manufactured in the course of its bitter struggles with the ruling bloc of imperial Britain.[75] There was already a long-standing reservoir of racialized representations circulating that included scientific theories, myths, stereotypes and narratives about others that could be picked up by any political actor. Such racism of the fin de siècle era was a common cultural inheritance, and no class was immunised against it.

But what was significant about Labour Party expressions of support for racism and empire was that they emanated from a political organisation that claimed to represent the working class. In the eyes of that class, it gave such statements a degree of authenticity, and therefore legitimacy, which consolidated the efforts made by the ruling elites to integrate them through relentless propaganda drives and invention of national traditions. Therefore, while framing their demands for class, country and empire allowed the Labour Party to 'speak beyond the margins of sectional interest', it also helped solidify racism and imperialism such that they became organic components of working-class culture.

The Fabian advocacy of social imperialism helped build a consensus across the Labour–Liberal divide that the state had an important role to play in uplifting all members of the so-called British imperial race. Such sentiment was further consolidated by the social investigations documenting poverty in London and York conducted by Charles Booth and Seebohm Rowntree. And this desire to maintain the empire combined with the recognition that this new racist-imperialist Labour Party posed a genuine threat to their electoral fortunes was sufficient to convince the 1906 Liberal government led by Lloyd George into initiating a series of social welfare reforms. These measures were devised to both prevent any further fragmentation of its working-class vote to the Labour Party and to uplift the 'race' for its imperial mission. Winston Churchill would later confirm that the taxes and resources of colonised subjects were the 'keystone' to such domestic welfare provision, helping to 'defray social services at a level incomparably higher than that of any European country'.[76]

Some of the more important items of legislation introduced included compensation for injury at work, the provision of free school meals, and medical inspections in schools. Pensions of between one and five shillings a week were also granted to those aged 70 and over. With the Labour Party increasing its parliamentary representation to 40 at the 1910 General Election, it began to behave 'less like an opposition party than as a pressure group',[77] pressing the Liberal Party to introduce further redistributive measures. From the delayed People's Budget of 1909, the Liberal-led coalition government responded by introducing the right to sick pay, free medical treatment and unemployment benefit in exchange for contributions to national insurance.[78]

The Labour Party as the second hegemonic project of the British state

The consolidation of the Labour Party as the primary political vehicle for the social and economic upliftment of the working class of Britain was the fortuitous product of contingent circumstances. It may well have remained a relatively minor centrist formation pressing the Liberal Party to further ameliorate the conditions of the labouring poor had it not been for three interlocking developments that helped sever working-class ties to the Liberal Party.

The first was the re-emergence of working-class militancy between 1911 and 1913. The Great Unrest involved more than 3,000 strikes with the number of days lost to strike action increasing from 4,576,000 days per year between 1900 and 1910 to 20,908,000 days per year between 1911 and 1913. Similarly, the number of workers involved in strike action increased from 240,000 per year between 1900 and 1910 to 1,034,000 per year between 1911 and 1913.[79] What such autonomous class action indicated was the widespread working-class discontent at the slow pace of democratic change and suspicion about the Janus-like character of the Liberal government. After all, the social welfare reforms had been accompanied by the Osborne judgment – a court ruling that required trade union members to 'contract in' if they wanted a portion of their salary to go towards a trade union. It was a measure effectively aimed at depriving the Labour Party of funds to pursue its political activities.

Just a year into the First World War, acquiescent elements of the working class also began to extricate themselves from the ideological stranglehold of Liberal hegemony. In February 1915, steep rises in the cost of living led 10,000 engineering workers in Glasgow to take unofficial action in support of increased wages and they were soon joined by miners from South Wales. When an attempt was made by trade union leaders and employers to make strike action illegal, the workers of Clydeside established their own organisation – the Clyde Workers' Committee – that declared: 'We will support the officials as long as they represent the workers, but we will act independently immediately they misrepresent them.'[80]

Second, accompanying this wave of industrial action was the growing militancy of the women's suffrage movement. While the first Women's Suffrage Committee was established in 1866, it was not until the founding of the National Union of Women's Suffrage Societies (NUWSS) in 1897 and the Women's Social and Political Union (WSPU) in 1903 that a mass movement for female suffrage began to assert its power in the democratic political process. The NUWSS was a mainly middle-class formation led by upper-class women like Millicent Fawcett, while the WSPU, led by Emmeline Pankhurst and Christabel Pankhurst, tended to have a more working-class base. While the NUWSS deployed conventional action repertoires such as marches, petitions and the lobbying of MPs, the WSPU's motto was 'deeds not words' and focused on a sustained campaign of civil disobedience that ranged from hunger strikes to arson attacks on property. Further, through organisations like the Women's Cooperative Guild and the Women's Trade Union Association, activists like Annie Kenney, Sarah Reddish, Ada Nield Chew and Selina Cooper helped entangle this demand for female enfranchisement with the ongoing labour unrest. Throughout this period, socialist newspapers carried articles on the subject of the women's vote, while women mobilised at union meetings with the Lancashire cotton mills being a particular stronghold.

It was amid this overlapping rebellion of the working class and women that the third factor – the outbreak of the First World War – intervened. A resurgence of nationalist fervour fractured both the women's and working-class movements. Nevertheless, their participation and sacrifice in the war effort, combined with elite concern about the possible re-emergence of a unified insurgent working-class revolt, led them to concede further reforms. A Speakers Conference was established in 1916 which eventually led to the enactment of the 1918 Representation of the People Act enfranchising 8.5 million women over the age of 30 and around 5.6 million men over the age of 21.[81]

While the electorate increased from around eight million to 22 million, it remained a gendered and 'property-based' parliamentary democracy. As Anna Muggeridge has demonstrated, two million of the poorest women over the age of 30 were excluded from the electoral rolls because of the requirement to be a property owner or local rates payer along with five million women aged between 21 and 30.[82] Effectively, the ruling bloc of Liberals and Conservatives took advantage of the class splits in the women's movement, with figures like Emmeline and Christabel Pankhurst employing a patriotic feminism to further the campaign for female citizenship during the war[83] and the upper-class women of the NUWSS offering no objections to the age and property restrictions.

In this way, the more radical dimension of the working-class women's struggle for gender and class justice was marginalised. And working-class women understood that all too well. Laura Schwartz, analysing female domestic servants' correspondence in journals such as *Common Cause*, found that they were not afraid to point out 'the hypocrisy of those claiming to fight for women's emancipation while benefitting from the exploitation of women workers in their own home'.[84] It would lead Sylvia Pankhurst to establish the East London Federation of the Suffragettes to draw working-class women back into struggle by linking the right to vote with better working conditions. But

they would have to wait until the 1928 Representation of
the People Act for electoral equality with men when all
women over 21 were enfranchised regardless of property
qualifications. Finally, at least within its domestic boundaries, the imperial state of Britain had become a genuine
parliamentary democracy.

While the Liberal-Conservative government led by Lloyd
George had hoped such democratic reforms would undercut
support for the Labour Party, they actually strengthened it.
There was a cornucopia of socialist currents that shaped the
class and gender struggles of the fin de siècle period, including
the internationalists of the Socialist League and the Socialist
Labour Party, syndicalists, Irish republicans and Jewish self-
organised groups. Yet they were never able to become the
hegemonic force in the field of politics. Instead, it would be
the Labour Party and its British national consciousness that
would emerge as the dominant influence. Through participation in the struggles across England, Scotland and Wales,
socialist activists came to understand that their class foe was
an integrated British ruling elite and that its power would be
most effectively challenged if it organised itself on the same
territorial footing. An early reflection of this realisation was
how influential Scottish socialists like James Maxton came to
reject any specificity of the Scottish struggle, instead locating
it within a British-wide campaign.[85] Further evidence of this
growing identification with Britishness within the working
class was the unthinking ease with which the first five leaders
of the Labour Party – all born in Scotland – were accepted as
leaders of a British-wide labour movement.

What this shows is how an understanding of socialism was
now increasingly bound up with ideas of British national
belonging. The social welfare and democratic reforms secured
by large parts of the working class in this period helped accelerate their incremental integration into the imperial state. In
essence, such reforms represented some of the final pieces
of the jigsaw through which much of the working class of
Britain voluntarily succumbed to the message that the British

nation was their nation, embedding this attachment deep in its collective consciousness such that it became part of its habitus. The granting of universal suffrage in 1928 was simply the formal ratification of this change in consciousness and understanding.

The hitherto 'unrespectable' working class now joined its 'respectable' cousin and found itself relentlessly drawn into the ever more complex web of British civil society. The sub-liminal message expressed through institutional mechanisms in the fields of culture and politics told the working class that 'you belong, that we have a responsibility to educate, clothe and feed you', and 'that you are an integral member of the superior race that rules the world'. And this bound them, at least in their imagination, to their British masters. The working class had travelled a long and difficult path since the Chartist demands for manhood suffrage. They were now active citizens of an imperial Britain with full political representation in Parliament.

A not insignificant consequence of this increasingly nationalised class struggle was that it strengthened the legit-imacy of the British state and the dominant rule of the cap-italist class. The effects of such integrative measures were to neutralise potentially powerful working-class opposition to the elites at home, while actively engaging this class in defence of Britain's imperialist mission abroad. Ernest Renan, the noted French historian and philosopher, once remarked that nations are built on 'collective forgetting'. In this instance, the working class had been invited to forget the contentious history of class war that had raged at regular intervals between themselves and their rulers since the 1780s. In place of these histories of shared struggle, they re-imagined themselves afresh as integral members of an imperial nation united by race.

The co-ordinates of British working-class politics were now set and would follow a trajectory where the class struggle would be contained within the boundaries of the nation-state. Two distinctive power blocs would dominate politics for the remainder of the twentieth century: first, the Conservative-led project of imperial nationalism and the second, a counter-hegemonic bloc comprising Labourite nationalism conjoined to social imperialism. The long-desired aim to democratise the British political system had been achieved, but at a cost, in so far as it bound the working class ever more closely to the politics of British nationalism, and a shared commitment to racism and empire. Over the course of the first half of the twentieth century, much of the British working class became increasingly adept at displaying a more open enthusiasm for empire than hitherto, drawn into a world of white superiority that had begun to exercise a magical hold over their imagination. And despite the continuing antipathy between the social classes, there was now little to distinguish their mental conceptions of race, nation and empire. Working-class demands for democratisation of the British political system were increasingly expressed and, indeed, legitimated, in opposition to the 'non-white' African and Asian beyond its internal borders, just as they were already being legitimated in opposition to the Jewish enemy within. Through such racialized narratives of re-imagining, much of the British population came to know themselves afresh – as a white, Christian people. Some, though not all, of the key material and symbolic elements of a lasting democratic settlement were now in place.

Notes

1 By democratisation, we refer to the 'net shift toward citizenship, breadth of citizenship, equality of citizenship, binding consultation, and protection'. Charles Tilly, 'Democratization: Working Paper', *Institute of Governmental Studies* 98, no. 7 (1998): 3.

2 Bob Jessop, 'The Capitalist State and the Rule of Capital: Problems in the Analysis of Business Associations', *West European Politics* 6, no. 2 (1983): 139–62.

3 Tilly, 'Democratization: Working Paper', 3.

4 Eric Williams, *Capitalism and Slavery* (London: Deutsch, 1964), 10.

5 Joseph E. Inikori, *Africans and the Industrial Revolution in England: A Study in International Trade and Economic Development* (Cambridge: Cambridge University Press, 2002).

6 Henry Heller, *The Birth of Capitalism: A 21st Century Perspective – the Future of World Capitalism* (London: Pluto Press, 2011), 197–98.

7 John Fielden cited in Karl Marx, *Capital*, vol. 1 (London: Penguin, 1990), 923.

8 Peter Linebaugh, *Red Round Globe Hot Burning: A Tale at the Crossroads of Commons and Closure, of Love and Terror, of Race and Class, and of Kate and Ned Despard* (Oakland: University of California Press, 2019).

9 Edward Palmer Thompson, *The Making of the English Working Class* (London: Penguin, 1991).

10 Satnam Virdee, *Racism, Class and the Racialized Outsider* (London: Palgrave Macmillan, 2014), 22–26.

11 Virdee, *Racism, Class and the Racialized Outsider*, 25.

12 C. L. R. James, *The Black Jacobins: Toussaint L'Ouverture and the San Domingo Revolution* (London: Penguin, 2001).

13 Thompson, *The Making of the English Working Class*, 80.

14 Thompson, *The Making of the English Working Class*, 109.

15 Virdee, *Racism, Class and the Racialized Outsider*, 22–26.

16 Thompson, *The Making of the English Working Class*, 123.

17 Virdee, *Racism, Class and the Racialized Outsider*, 26–31.

18 Cited in Virdee, *Racism, Class and the Racialized Outsider*, 30.

19 John Belchem, 'English Working-Class Radicalism and the Irish, 1815–50', in *The Irish in the Victorian City*, edited by Roger Swift and Sheridan Gilley (London: Routledge, 1985), 93.

20 Belchem, 'English Working-Class Radicalism and the Irish', 94.

21 Perry Anderson, 'Origins of the Present Crisis', *New Left Review* 1, no. 23 (1964): 33.

22 Anderson, 'Origins of the Present Crisis', 36.

23 Eric J. Hobsbawm, *The Age of Capital 1848–1875* (London: Abacus, 1997), 134.

24 Robert Saunders, 'The Politics of Reform and the Making of the Second Reform Act, 1848–1867', *The Historical Journal* 50, no. 3 (2007): 578.

25 Lowe cited in Saunders, 'The Politics of Reform and the Making of the Second Reform Act', 582.

26 Gladstone cited in Saunders, 'The Politics of Reform and the Making of the Second Reform Act', 582.

27 Eric J. Hobsbawm, *Industry and Empire: From 1750 to the Present Day* (London: Penguin, 1990), 126.

28 Gladstone cited in Saunders, 'The Politics of Reform and the Making of the Second Reform Act', 582.

29 Hobsbawm, *The Age of Capital 1848–1875*, 263.

30 Reginald Horsman, 'Origins of Racial Anglo-Saxonism in Great Britain Before 1850', *Journal of the History of Ideas* 37, no. 3 (1976): 398–99.

31 Robbie Shilliam, *Race and the Undeserving Poor: From Abolition to Brexit* (Newcastle upon Tyne: Agenda Publishing, 2018); Catherine Hall, 'Rethinking Imperial Histories: The Reform Act of 1867', *New Left Review* 1, no. 208 (1994): 3–29.

32 Virdee, *Racism, Class and the Racialized Outsider.*

33 Linda Colley, *Britons: Forging the Nation, 1707–1837* (London: Vintage, 1996).

34 Robert J. C. Young, *The Idea of English Ethnicity* (Oxford: Blackwell Publishing, 2007).

35 John Saville, *1848: The British State and the Chartist Movement* (Cambridge: Cambridge University Press, 1987), 38.

36 L. Perry Curtis, *Anglo-Saxons and Celts: A Study of Anti-Irish Prejudice in Victorian England* (New York: New York University Press, 1968). See also Young, *The Idea of English Ethnicity.*

37 Hall, 'Rethinking Imperial Histories', 10.

38 Edmond Beales cited in Alex Middleton, 'The Second Reform Act and the Politics of Empire', *Parliamentary History* 36, no. 1 (2017): 87.

39 Shilliam, *Race and the Undeserving Poor: From Abolition to Brexit.*

40 Cited in Hall, 'Rethinking Imperial Histories', 22.

41 Cited in Shilliam, *Race and the Undeserving Poor: From Abolition to Brexit*, 45.

42 Cited in Hall, 'Rethinking Imperial Histories', 17.

43 R. H. Hutton cited in Hall, 'Rethinking Imperial Histories', 19.

44 Benjamin Disraeli, 'Parliamentary Reform – Representation of the People Bill – [Bill 237] – Third Reading (Hansard, 15 July 1867)', 1867, https://api.parliament.uk/historic-hansard/commons/1867/jul/15/parliamentary-reform-representation-of#S3V0188P0_18670715_HOC_87.

45 Disraeli cited in Horsman, 'Origins of Racial Anglo-Saxonism in Great Britain Before 1850', 404.

46 Benjamin Disraeli, 'Parliamentary Reform – Representation of the People Bill – Leave, First Reading (Hansard, 18 March 1867)', 1867, https://api.parliament.uk/historic-hansard/commons/1867/mar/18/leave-first-reading#S3V0186P0_18670318_HOC_30.

47 Anderson, 'Origins of the Present Crisis'; Tom Nairn, 'The English Working Class', *New Left Review* 1, no. 24 (1964): 43–57.

48 Nairn, 'The English Working Class', 49.

49 Discourses of the French Revolution seeped into Britain to inform the activism of the Corresponding Societies while, closer to home, the socialism of Robert Owen crossed into England from Scotland to conjure up a utopian vision of social justice for all.

50 Virdee, *Racism, Class and the Racialized Outsider*.

51 The limited nature of this statute should be noted in so far as it excluded the majority of the male working class, women of all social classes as well as racialized minorities within the working class.

52 Hobsbawm, *Industry and Empire*, 124.

53 Gurminder K. Bhambra, 'Relations of Extraction, Relations of Redistribution: Empire, Nation, and the Construction of the British Welfare State', *The British Journal of Sociology* 73, no. 1 (2022): 8.

54 Matthew Roberts, 'Resisting "Arithmocracy": Parliament, Community, and the Third Reform Act', *Journal of British Studies* 50, no. 2 (2011): 391.

55 James D. Young, *The Rousing of the Scottish Working Class 1774–2008* (Glasgow: Clydeside Press, 2009).

56 Virdee, *Racism, Class and the Racialized Outsider*, 51.

57 William Knox, 'Religion and the Scottish Labour Movement, c.1900–1939', *Journal of Contemporary History* 23, no. 4 (1988): 626.

58 Knox, 'Religion and the Scottish Labour Movement', 609.

59 Reid cited in Knox, 'Religion and the Scottish Labour Movement', 616.

60 Cited in Virdee, *Racism, Class and the Racialized Outsider*, 146.

61 Daniel Renshaw, *Socialism and the Diasporic 'Other': A Comparative Study of Irish Catholic and Jewish Radical and Communal*

Politics in East London, 1889–1912 (Liverpool: Liverpool University Press, 2018).

62 Yet, the Labour Party never secured the assent of the majority of the working class until the 1945 General Election in large part because of the pre-existing current of Conservative imperial nationalism that had already sunk deep roots within significant parts of the Protestant working class.

63 Tillett cited in William J. Fishman, *East End Jewish Radicals 1875–1914* (Nottingham: Five Leaves Publications, 2004), 77.

64 Eric Hobsbawm, 'Trade Union History', *The Economic History Review* 20, no. 2 (1967): 359.

65 Ben Gray, 'Ben Tillett and the Rise of the Labour Movement in Britain', *History Review* 34 (1999): 4.

66 Tillett cited in Monty Meth, *Brothers to All Men? Report on Trade Union Actions and Attitudes on Race Relations* (London: The Runnymede Trust, 1972), 5.

67 Claire Hirshfield, 'The British Left and the "Jewish Conspiracy": A Case Study of Modern Antisemitism', *Jewish Social Studies* 43, no. 2 (1981): 97.

68 Virdee, *Racism, Class and the Racialized Outsider*. For a discussion of antisemitism and the socialist movement across Europe during this period, see B. McGeever and S. Virdee, 'Antisemitism and Socialist Strategy in Europe, 1880–1917: An Introduction', *Patterns of Prejudice* 51, no. 3–4 (2017): 221–34.

69 Virdee, *Racism, Class and the Racialized Outsider*, 51.

70 Keith Laybourn, 'The Failure of Socialist Unity in Britain c. 1893–1914', *Transactions of the Royal Historical Society* 4 (1994): 158.

71 Ralph Miliband, *Parliamentary Socialism: A Study in the Politics of Labour* (London: Merlin Press, 1987).

72 Partha Sarathi Gupta, *Imperialism and the British Labour Movement, 1914–1964* (New York: Holmes and Meier Publishers, 1975); Alan M. McBriar, *Fabian Socialism and English Politics, 1884–1918* (Cambridge: Cambridge University Press, 1963).

73 Jonathan Rose, *The Intellectual Life of the British Working Classes* (New Haven: Yale University Press, 2002).

74 Gupta, *Imperialism and the British Labour Movement, 1914–1964*, 11.

75 Alastair Bonnett, *White Identities: An Historical & International Introduction* (London: Routledge, 1999).

76 Churchill cited in Bhambra, 'Relations of Extraction, Relations of Redistribution', 11.

77 Miliband, *Parliamentary Socialism*, 22.

78 James Roy Hay, *The Origins of the Liberal Welfare Reforms: 1906–1914* (London: Macmillan Education, 1987).

79 James Hinton and Richard Hyman, *Trade Unions and Revolution: The Industrial Politics of the Early British Communist Party* (London: Pluto Press, 1975), 15.

80 Virdee, *Racism, Class and the Racialized Outsider*, 76.

81 It was 19 if you had served in the military.

82 Anna Muggeridge, 'The Missing Two Million: The Exclusion of Working-Class Women from the 1918 Representation of the People Act', *Revue Française de Civilisation Britannique. French Journal of British Studies* 23, no. 1 (2018): xxiii–1; Hinton and Hyman, *Trade Unions and Revolution*, 15.

83 Mary Hilson, 'Women Voters and the Rhetoric of Patriotism in the British General Election of 1918', *Women's History Review* 10, no. 2 (2001): 325–47; Jo Vellacott, *Pacifists, Patriots and the Vote: The Erosion of Democratic Suffragism in Britain During the First World War* (New York: Palgrave Macmillan, 2007).

84 Laura Schwartz, *Feminism and the Servant Problem: Class and Domestic Labour in the Women's Suffrage Movement* (Cambridge: Cambridge University Press, 2019).

85 Young, *The Rousing of the Scottish Working Class 1774–2008*.

2   The underside of the welfare state

The 1945–51 Labour administration was 'the decisive happening in the history of Labourism'.[1] In contrast to the subsequent disappointments of the Wilson–Callaghan and Blair–Brown governments, the Attlee administration is held up to this day by Labour Party socialists as the archetype of the radical reforming government that transformed the everyday lives of working-class Britons.[2] It was undoubtedly a moment of significant working-class advancement exemplified by the newly established National Health Service, full employment and the guarantee of effective trade union rights. According to Tom Nairn,[3] the seeds of the welfare state were planted during the time of war when the Conservative and Labour parties came together in a government of national unity to thwart the threat of German National Socialist expansionism. It was then that it became possible to speak of a shared yet unthinking attachment to British national identity across all social classes in Scotland, England and Wales.

However, our longer historical arc offers a different interpretation of this period. We suggest it should be understood as the highpoint of the democratic settlement. It was not just a rare moment of social democratic hegemony but the culmination of a century of continuous incremental reform and working-class integration into the nation. Significantly, this post-war moment cannot be separated from the insoluble fact that Britain remained an imperial power, albeit a declining one. The inter-class truce would be resourced, in part, through the combined economic returns of empire abroad and the super-exploitation of migrant labour at home. Racism, as it had throughout the previous century, formed a constitutive feature of this final phase of the democratic settlement, helping to solidify colour-coded hierarchies of labour both within and beyond the boundaries of the British state.

Further, what distinguishes this culminating moment of the democratic settlement is that it coincided with the beginning of the end of the British empire. That is, the principal economic cornerstone, that 'indispensable cushion'[4] which opened the possibility of the incremental inclusion of the domestic working class into the British nation in the mid-nineteenth century starts to crack and crumble just as the final touches are put to the apotheosis of the domestic democratic settlement. The subsequent history of British politics along with the accompanying conflicts and fissures that would culminate in the Scottish independence referendum and Brexit are the convoluted artefact of the fundamental conundrum that has stumped the British state and its ruling class ever since: how to maintain its geopolitical influence and sustain the relative competitiveness of British capitalism in the aftermath of empire while continuing to deliver a level of social, economic and psychic security that could guarantee the maintenance of domestic social order. This chapter traces the twists and turns between the years of 1945 and 1970, particularly the contradictions and conflicts they produced, and the development of new strategies to maintain social order and capitalist rule.

Empire, racism and the reserve army of labour

According to James Vernon, 'the political economy of social democracy was no less embedded in imperial and global structures'[5] than the Conservative and Liberal imperialisms that preceded it. Despite the loss of India in August 1947, the Labour government remained resolutely opposed to relinquishing the empire, understanding it as the fundamental economic cornerstone of British capitalism guaranteeing geopolitical power and the expansion of the domestic welfare state. Like previous Liberal and Conservative imperialists before him, Labour leaders like Ernest Bevin, then Foreign Secretary, imagined Britain at the epicentre of 'a great Empire and Commonwealth of Nations, which touches all parts of the world, and which will have to deal ... with every race'.[6]

He insisted that Britain could retain its position as a world power alongside the United States and the Soviet Union, informing Hugh Dalton, then Chancellor of the Exchequer, of his intention 'to organise the middle of the Planet', encompassing Western Europe, the Mediterranean, the Middle East and the Commonwealth: 'If we only push on and develop Africa, we could have [the] US dependent on us, and eating out of our hand, in four or five years. Two great mountains of manganese ore in Sierra Leone, etc. US is very barren of essential minerals, and in Africa we have them all.'[7]

Further, for Bevin as well as other Labour ministers, domestic economic reconstruction including the establishment of the welfare state was explicitly tied to the maintenance of Britain's colonies. 'I am not prepared to sacrifice the British Empire ... because I know that if the British Empire fell ... it would mean the standard of life of our constituents would fall considerably.'[8] As far as the leadership of the Labour Party were concerned, the imperial dividend was 'integral to the construction of the post-war welfare state'.[9] Or as Labour MP John Strachey put it, the primary extraction of resources from the colonies 'by one means or another, by hook or by crook ... is a life and death matter for the economy of the country'.[10] And to secure this objective, the post-war Labour government was more than willing to play a counter-revolutionary role by repressing communists leading national liberation struggles in Britain's colonies. They understood that 'the flexibility and manoeuvrability of the ruling class ... was derived from the possession of the world's largest empire'.[11]

And for much of the two decades after the Second World War, successive Labour and Conservative administrations proved unwilling to relinquish it, particularly those parts of the empire like Malaya and Ghana that remained profitable. When riots erupted in Accra, Ghana, in February 1948, British forces imprisoned Kwame Nkrumah, the leader of the Convention People's Party,[12] while in Malaya, Britain went to war with those forces loyal to the Malayan Communist Party in the same year. Rita Hinden, head of the Fabian Colonial Bureau, claimed, 'We have not the intention ... of sacrificing our standard of living for the sake of colonial development, we do not contemplate an evening out of wealth; we know, too, that our development plans are partly inspired by our own needs.'[13]

And such arguments were accompanied by a thinly veiled racism directed at anti-colonial leaders that suggested 'the transfer of power was going to be contingent on the rate of social and economic progress in colonial territories'.[14] An affinity with the socialist principle of international working-class solidarity was absent among this post-war generation of Labour and trade union leaders.[15] Instead, most deployed a racialized and hierarchical understanding of labour, with the domestic working class to be guaranteed a degree of economic and political security by increasing the rate of exploitation of black and brown workers across the remaining parts of empire, particularly in Africa.

If retaining those parts of the empire that remained profitable was one aspect of the post-war Labour strategy to rebuild Britain and expand the welfare state, then the other was its importation of a reserve army of labour to resolve the crisis of profitability facing parts of British industry as it became less competitive in the world market. In an environment where it was claimed that 'you couldn't get an armless, legless man, never mind an able-bodied one',[16] the Attlee administration granted the right of settlement to over 100,000 members of the Polish Armed Forces who had been in exile in Britain since the start of the Second World War. Between October 1946 and December 1949, a further 80,000 European Volunteer Workers were recruited from Displaced Persons Camps in Germany and Austria.[17] This was supplemented by the arrival of between 70,000 and 100,000 people from the Republic of Ireland.[18] Employers also widened their search with the British Hotels and Restaurant Association, London Transport and the National Health Service actively recruiting in the colonies. Between 1948 and 1961, these initiatives alongside the continuing shortages of labour in heavy manufacturing industry encouraged more than 400,000 workers from the Caribbean and the Indian sub-continent to join the migrant labour force that was arriving from Europe.[19]

Caribbean and Asian workers settled in Britain amid the apex of an unprecedented inter-class truce characterised by the large-scale horizontal integration of the working class into the imagined national community. This period is today celebrated as the golden age of social democracy portrayed in Ken Loach's 2013 film *The Spirit of '45*. Yet when interrogated through the eyes of Caribbean and Asian workers, it is more appropriately understood as a catastrophe. Attachment to the twin racializing projects of imperial and socialist nationalism was so comprehensive that there was simply no institutional space in British political culture to make sense of the Caribbean and Asian presence from a progressive standpoint. Just two days after the *Empire Windrush* docked in Tilbury on 22 June 1948 – carrying 493 migrants from Jamaica – eleven Labour MPs wrote to the Prime Minister, Clement Attlee, calling for the restriction of black immigration on the grounds that '[a]n influx of coloured people domiciled here is likely to impair the harmony, strength and cohesion of our public and social life and to cause discord and unhappiness among all concerned'.[20]

An increasingly racialized debate on immigration unfolded, 'focusing on the supposed social problems of having too many black immigrants and the question of how they could be stopped from entering, given their legal rights under the 1948 British Nationality Act'.[21] And it continued throughout the 1950s, with Churchill trying to convince his cabinet to adopt the slogan 'Keep England White' at the forthcoming General Election of 1955[22] on the grounds that restricting Caribbean migration was 'the most important subject facing this country'.[23] By the mid-1950s, both Labour and Conservative governments had 'instituted a number of covert and sometimes illegal, administrative measures designed to discourage black immigration'.[24]

Alongside such party political and state racism, Caribbean and Asian workers were confronted with practices of social closure from parts of the organised working class, who in opposition to their presence came to re-imagine themselves as white. Major workplaces like Ford Dagenham, British Railways, Vickers, Napiers and Tate & Lyle operated colour bars enforced by trade unions. The closed shop principle was used by trade unionists to limit Caribbean and Asian access to skilled work. The use of discriminatory practices was particularly evident in transport, textiles and foundry work where white trade unionists resisted the employment of black workers or insisted on a quota system limiting them to around 5 per cent of the workforce. If such informal agreements were breached by employers, wildcat strikes were initiated to bring them back into line – a sort of DIY racism which helped enforce a hierarchical ordering of the working class based on colour.[25]

In February 1955, in the West Midlands, employees of the West Bromwich Corporation Transport system began a series of Saturday strikes in protest against the employment of an Indian trainee conductor. In the same year, transport workers in Wolverhampton banned all overtime in protest at the increasing employment of black labour, and the breaching of the 5 per cent quota for black workers. In this period, the long-standing principle of 'last in first out' when redundancies were threatened was abandoned if it meant white workers would lose their jobs before black workers. As one official of a general union confirmed: 'in the event of redundancy occurring his members would insist on coloured workers going first'.[26] Racism and empire were integral to securing this post-war inter-class settlement, helping to solidify 'identities, informal understandings, shared strategies and political collusion which linked the labour movement, government agencies and other prominent social institutions in a common, yet contradictory changing [alliance] against black workers'.[27]

The nationalisation of the Communist Party of Great Britain

During this period, the movement for socialism came to be associated not just with the Labour Party but also the Communist Party of Great Britain (CPGB), whose membership had increased to 45,435 by 1945.[28] Alongside a strong industrial presence, the re-election of Willie Gallacher in West Fife in 1945 and the addition of Phil Piratin as MP for Mile End gave the party a modest national profile. However, having endorsed the programme for a parliamentary road to socialism in 1951, it located its vision for socialist transformation on the same ideological terrain of British nationalism as the Labour Party. It thereby found itself trapped in a bind of its own making. Challenging racism directed against black and Asian workers would have required it to also challenge the British nationalism that legitimated such discrimination. But this would have undermined the logic of the CPGB's own perspective of achieving socialism in Britain. Unable to summon the spirit of socialist internationalism for fear it would clash with its commitment to a more 'respectable' politics of forging 'broad democratic alliances', the CPGB found itself incapable of effectively countering the mounting racism faced by black and Asian workers from parts of the white working class. Its elementary understanding of such racism as a form of historical residue rooted in colonial oppression ignored the conditions for its contemporary reproduction in Britain. This further 'served to reinforce the "foreignness" of immigrant workers'[29] and give credence to the idea that they

didn't belong in Britain. With the elimination of racism tied to
a 'long-term programme of colonial freedom',[30] all the CPGB
could offer in the interim were moral platitudes, grounding its
objection to racism and 'colour bars' with reference to abstract
arguments about the intrinsic unity of the human race.[31]

   This is not to deny the existence of a minority current
of organised opposition to racism, discrimination and
empire throughout the different stages of Britain's democratic settlement.[32] In her landmark book *Insurgent Empire*,
Priyamvada Gopal reminds us 'The history of the British Empire
is also the history of resistance to it. And importantly, from both
beyond and within Britain.'[33] And it is the case that even during
the 1950s and 1960s, there were racialized minorities within the
CPGB, men and women like Ranji Chadrasingh and Claudia
Jones who conducted indispensable work in drawing attention
to the plight of Caribbean and Asian workers in Britain and its
colonies. Jones, in particular, played an instrumental part in the
West Indian Workers and Students Association, as well as in
establishing the *West Indian Gazette*, Britain's first major black
newspaper in 1958.[34] She campaigned tirelessly for equality
in education, employment and housing.[35] Overall, however,
the contribution of the CPGB as a political formation in challenging racism was disappointing, contributing to the loss of
key black activists like Trevor Carter and Frank Bailey. The
latter would ruefully remind socialists how 'the British labour
movement, neither Right nor Left had never done anything for
the colonial liberation movement'.[36]

Decolonisation abroad, the intensification of racism at home

As the struggles for national self-determination intensified
throughout the British empire over the course of the 1950s,
they added further fuel to the rising arc of racist reaction
within Britain itself. The Conservatives, first under Churchill
and then Eden, had come to power still unwilling to relinquish those colonies that remained profitable, regarding them

as crucial to sustaining Britain's dominant position in the post-war world order. At the same time, Britain's declining imperial reach was exposed by its seeming inability to repress movements for national independence in Kenya, Malaya and elsewhere. The nadir for empire advocates came in 1956, when the Egyptian nationalist, Abdul Gamal Nasser, unilaterally nationalised the Suez Canal. Having already lost India, the canal was seen as crucial to maintaining Britain's preeminent position in the Middle East and Asia. When Britain, along with France, colluded with Israel to engineer an attack on Egypt and retake the canal, the US government refused to back the invasion. UN intervention and US pressure forced Britain into a humiliating withdrawal of its forces, hastening Eden's resignation in 1957. This episode had a devastating effect on British national confidence; symbolically, it marked the end of the British empire.[37]

Carefully cultivated over three centuries, the empire crumpled like a deck of cards in the face of a sustained cycle of anti-colonial resistance. From the civil disobedience movement that secured India's independence in 1947 to the domino-like collapse of the British Caribbean – Jamaica in 1962; Trinidad and Tobago in 1962; Barbados in 1966; and Guyana in 1966 – a mood of global rebellion was in the air. The revolutionary fervour forced the then Prime Minister Harold Macmillan to underscore the inevitable 'wind of change' that heralded the demise of empire. Between the election of the Attlee government in 1945 and the Wilson government in October 1964, the number of people under British rule fell from 700 million to five million (of whom three million were in Hong Kong alone).[38]

Within Britain itself, the reaction to this unprecedented defeat added new ingredients to an already toxic cocktail of racist sentiment and discrimination directed at black and Asian workers. Unable to prevent the loss of empire to the 'dark hordes' of Africa and Asia, these empire loyalists now projected their racism on to those Asian and Caribbean workers in Britain. In the summer of 1958, racist riots

erupted in Nottingham in the East Midlands and Notting
Hill, west London. On successive nights, hundreds of white
people gathered on the streets of St. Ann's in Nottingham
looking for black people to attack. In Notting Hill, white
working-class youths attacked black people with iron bars,
butchers' knives and weighted leather belts demanding 'Keep
Britain White'. The first night of racist violence left five black
men unconscious on the pavements.[39]

Britain was witnessing the 'restaging of the colonial
encounter',[40] but this time at home with black and brown
migrants in Britain in the crosshairs of an unprecedented wave
of racist reaction. In the absence of any significant organised
opposition to such racism, the political elites moved quickly
towards limiting the entry of black and brown workers.
By 1962, the journey of transforming British Caribbean
and Asian populations from 'citizens into migrants'[41] was
instigated with the introduction of the Commonwealth
Immigrants Act. While the Conservative government was
at pains to stress at the time that the statute was not racist,
the then minister without portfolio – William Deedes –
conceded many years later that the legislation had indeed
been intended 'to restrict the influx of coloured immigrants'.
He continued: 'we were reluctant to say as much openly. So,
the restrictions were applied to coloured and white citizens in
all Commonwealth countries – though everybody recognised
that immigration from Canada, Australia and New Zealand
formed no part of the problem.'[42]

Cracks in the consensus I: state attacks, working-class resistance

By the mid-1960s, two of the formative strategies employed
by the ruling class to maintain the profitability of British
capitalism while supporting an expanding welfare state had
ground to a shuddering halt. Alongside the end of empire, its
efforts to construct a racialized division of labour through the

importation of a super-exploited reserve army of labour from the Caribbean and the Indian sub-continent had been curtailed by the intensification of popular racisms, culminating in the passing of the 1962 Commonwealth Immigrants Act.

At the same time, the fundamental problems of British capitalism remained: archaic imperial structures no longer fit for purpose, over-dependence on finance capital and signs of a decline in the productivity of British industry. Britain's democratic settlement was now in crisis. 'If the slide continued', argued Tom Nairn at the time, 'Britain would be relegated to a secondary, ultimately to a dependent position on the margins of the capitalist world ... there would be a relative decline in the standard of living, a final end to Britain's political and military significance and to that glorified second-best, the Commonwealth – and a permanent small-bit role on the world scene'.[43]

Both Conservative and Labour elites were aware of British capitalism's difficulties, particularly its relative decline compared to its Western European rivals.[44] No longer able to sustain its status as a global power, the Conservatives had applied for Britain to join the Common Market in 1961 – a move coincidentally sandwiched between Macmillan's 'wind of change' announcing the end of the British empire and the implementation of the Immigration Act limiting Caribbean and Asian migration. However, the application was vetoed by De Gaulle in 1963 and it would be another ten years before it was finally granted entry by which time Britain was commonly known as 'the sick man of Europe'.[45] Membership of this transnational union was an inherently contradictory project in so far as it could never replace the empire Britain had lost. Colonialism was undergirded by an unequal economic and political arrangement rooted in extraction and expropriation of wealth from the colonies back to Britain. The EU, on the other hand, was ostensibly a club of equals; states who had agreed voluntarily to pool individual national sovereignty to ensure continuing European capitalist supremacy and geopolitical influence. It simply wasn't designed to deliver

the sort of economic and social security that parts of the
working class of Britain had belatedly secured through the
economic returns of empire.[46]

It therefore became increasingly clear to Labour and
Conservative elites they would have to reverse key elements of the post-war democratic settlement to guarantee
the future competitiveness of British capitalism. And it
would be the incoming Labour government of 1964 led
by Harold Wilson that would make the first effort to curtail the power of organised labour. Portraying itself as 'the
party of the new, rationalised future',[47] Labour promised
to grow and modernise the British economy through its
advocacy of a 'neutral, "technocratic" ideal whose ultimate
ideal was the efficient and humane management of a permanent mixed economy'.[48] In 1965, as part of this modernisation process, it appointed a Royal Commission on Trade
Unions and Employer Associations under the chairmanship
of Lord Donovan to consider relations between management and trade unions. It identified two systems of industrial
relations: the formal system represented by industry-wide
collective agreements, and the informal system represented
by the actual behaviour of managers and workers at the
factory level. The Commission ruled that growing disorder
in the informal system was the central defect in British industrial relations responsible for harming the competitiveness of
British industry.

While it had been careful to identify poor management
as the principal culprit of this growing disorder, the Labour
government chose instead to focus on the ability of rank
and file trade union representatives to secure important
improvements in pay and conditions through the deployment of wildcat strikes. In an era of tight labour markets
and full employment, the workplace organiser came to be
'constructed as a symbol of trade union irresponsibility', such
that by 1969 the Labour government had released a white
paper, *In Place of Strife*, declaring its intention to use the law
to curb such localised conflict. This was nothing less than

an attempt to legally limit the ability of the working class to secure improved living conditions through autonomous collective action. While the Labour bill was defeated due to the pressure brought to bear on the government by the trade union movement, the incoming Conservative government of 1970 proceeded to pass the 1971 Industrial Relations Bill which replaced the collectivist laissez-faire system of industrial relations with a comprehensive legal framework designed to restrict industrial conflict.[49]

Such growing interventions by both Labour and Conservative governments in employer–labour relations stimulated a dramatic escalation in the class struggle. Significant elements of the organised working class recognised that living standards could no longer be maintained simply through the operation of closed shops and collective bargaining arrangements. Instead, there was an increasing turn towards taking collective action leading to the most significant class confrontations in more than half a century. The number of strike days rose dramatically from an average of less than four million days a year during the 1950s and 1960s to 24 million days in 1972 alone.[50] A significant proportion of these strikes were qualitatively different from those of the 1950s and 1960s, with 'a wide range of traditionally moderate and peaceful workers, many of them women, embarking on strike action, many for the first time in their lives'.[51] Attempts to curb unofficial strike activity also saw the return of the political strike for the first time since the 1920s. A series of one-day stoppages against the 1971 Industrial Relations Bill culminated in the TUC instructing its members to refuse to register as trade unions when the Bill became law. Such collective action was reinforced by over 500 occupations and sit-ins that took place during this period.[52]

The ramifications of such sustained resistance were dramatic. The long-held common-sense understanding of a shared national interest began to break down, as workers witnessed attempts by employers to enforce inferior living conditions. Significant elements of organised labour were drawn into the orbit of a socialist left to combat attempts to undermine working-class living standards. These activists refused to put a brake on workers' struggles, and instead encouraged such strikes. As this collective action grew exponentially throughout 1972[53] it signalled, above all, that many workers were increasingly looking beyond the conventional tactics employed to defend working-class conditions achieved during the apex of the age of democratic capitalism.[54]

Over time, this growing alignment between parts of the working class and socialist activists helped initiate the process of transforming the leadership of the trade union movement at all levels. It forced some traditional national trade union leaders to adopt a more combative class perspective, whilst others who refused to adapt to the changing relations of force were swept away in the maelstrom and replaced by left-wing leaders. Significant leftward swings in the leadership of several major trade unions took place during this period, including the Amalgamated Engineering Union, the Transport and General Workers Union (TGWU) and the General, Municipal and Boilermakers' Union.[55]

At the district, regional and shop steward level, it brought to positions of influence a diverse layer of socialist activists, including left-wingers in the Labour Party, members of the CPGB, as well as representatives from various Trotskyist organisations. By the mid-1970s, it was estimated that 10 per cent of all trade union officials were communists of one kind or another.[56] This wave of industrial struggle arrested the CPGB's long-term decline in membership[57] while various Trotskyist parties saw notable increases in their membership,[58] with the most significant of them – the International Socialists – growing from around 1,000 members across 47 branches to around 3,500 members with some implantation in the organised working class.[59]

The loss of empire and the curtailment of a racialized reserve army of labour had inaugurated a crisis of the democratic settlement. In trying to resolve the dilemma of ensuring the profitability of post-imperial British capitalism alongside the maintenance of domestic social order, successive Labour and Conservative governments ended up deepening the crisis of the British social formation. Under sustained assault from both political parties, sections of the organised working class began to increasingly act autonomously in defence of their working conditions.

Cracks in the consensus II: the politics of Powellism

While the Labour government had moved quickly to reassure the public of its intention to retain the 1962 Commonwealth Immigrants Act, it was also keen to ensure that Britain remained at the epicentre of the postcolonial Commonwealth. This was essential for the ruling elites if Britain was to maintain its historically expansive geopolitical reach and the profitability of British capitalism.[60] It was this instrumentalised concern that brought about a change in Labour policy. Following negative international publicity brought to bear by the West Indian Development Council-led boycott of the Bristol Omnibus Company for their refusal to employ black and Asian bus crews, the Labour government was forced into tackling some of the more explicit dimensions of structural racism. The resulting 1965 Race Relations Act not only outlawed discrimination in public places like hotels and restaurants, but also established the Race Relations Board (RRB) and the National Committee for Commonwealth Immigrants (NCCI) to further the objective of racial equality.

Shortly thereafter, a study commissioned by the RRB and NCCI found that while Caribbeans, Indians and Pakistanis occupied a diversity of class positions in their countries of origin, they had undergone an undifferentiated process of proletarianisation in Britain. Investigating the causes of such downward social mobility, Daniel found that 'a very substantial proportion of coloured people claim experience of discrimination ... their claims are largely justified and ... it is the most able ones [i.e. white-collar workers] that experience most discrimination'.[61] The study demonstrated conclusively that in 1960s Britain, racist discrimination ranged from the 'massive to the substantial'.[62] It found an informal colour bar in operation, which, while 'more covert and insidious than that operated in some other societies with different legal status for people of different colours ... [was] nonetheless effective, and perhaps even more distressing, for that'.[63] In sum, the outcome of nearly two decades of systematic racist discrimination had helped produce two working classes, one white and the other black, hierarchically ordered and politically constituted in opposition to one another.

Faced with such compelling evidence, the Labour government introduced a more comprehensive Race Relations Act in 1968 that made it illegal to refuse housing, employment or public services to individuals because of their 'racial' background. The Act would also go on to extend the powers of the Race Relations Board and establish the Community Relations Commission, which aimed at promoting 'racial harmony' among different communities. In introducing these pieces of legislation, Labour was adopting a contradictory programme of support for racist immigration controls on the one hand, and the promise of racial equality on the other. It would become a recurring feature of its stance over the subsequent decades and was neatly encapsulated by Roy Hattersley (a former Home Office minister) in his formulation 'Integration without control is impossible, but control without integration is indefensible.'[64]

The Conservative right, particularly a significant element of its activist and voting base, were outraged. Having already compelled the then Labour Home Secretary, James Callaghan, to introduce emergency legislation to end the right of East African Asians from entering Britain lawfully (as British citizens) in early 1968,[65] they now turned their anger towards the Asian and Caribbean populations already settled in Britain. On Saturday 20 April 1968, Enoch Powell, MP for Wolverhampton South-West, and shadow defence spokesman under Edward Heath, delivered a speech to an audience of 85 Conservatives in a second-floor meeting room of the Midland Hotel in Birmingham.[66] Employing emotive anecdotes to highlight the dangers of black and Asian settlement in Britain, he claimed: 'I simply do not have the right to shrug my shoulders and think about something else' when some areas 'are already undergoing the total transformation to which there is no parallel in a thousand years of English history'.[67] 'We must be mad, literally mad, as a nation to be permitting the annual inflow of some 50,000 dependents, who are for the most part the material of the future growth of the immigrant descended population. It is like watching a nation busily engaged in heaping up its own funeral pyre.'[68]

In Powell's mind, having already lost the empire, Labour was now effectively recognising the existence of black and brown Britons and their right to expect equal treatment under the law by introducing such anti-discrimination legislation. For Powell, the former arch-imperialist, this would effectively decouple the long association of whiteness with Britishness that had been so successful in cementing unity across social classes in pursuit of the state's imperialist ambitions abroad and the maintenance of hegemony at home. According to this racializing logic, black and Asian workers had now become the unwanted reminder of peoples abroad who wanted nothing to do with the British empire. And, in the mind of Powell, this invited the question, 'What are they doing here in Britain?'

The logic underpinning this racism, however, was now no longer designed to unify the nation with a view to recapturing its lost empire. Powell was politically astute enough to realise that the empire was gone forever. Significantly, he also believed that Labour and the Conservatives were delusional to think that the Commonwealth could serve as a mechanism for consolidating global trading relationships initially forged through colonisation. Such an approach, he believed, risked giving credibility to demands that Britain redistribute its resources to the former colonies.[69] Instead, the intention of this new racism was to expunge all memory of the empire and Commonwealth from Britain's national story, to redefine British 'national identity in terms appropriate to the times – and in particular, appropriate to the end of empire'.[70] Only then could Britain recover from the stupor into which it had fallen as a result of the wind of change that had brought forth decolonisation.

This was why Powell focused his anger and resentment towards the Asian and Caribbean populations that arrived between 1948 and 1962, together with their British-born children. In his mind, they represented the living embodiment of the empire now lost, a painful and daily reminder of their defeat on the world stage. England's rebirth was made dependent on their expulsion to their ancestral lands of origin. Powell was offering a powerful re-imagining of the English nation after empire, reminding his audience it was a nation for whites only.

While the national political debate became increasingly refracted through the prism of racism, it is important not to separate this discussion from the wider economic difficulties facing the British ruling elites in the aftermath of empire, and how they tried to resolve them. Valuable new interpretations of this period demonstrate that this insular racializing nationalism was intimately entwined with Powell's support for what would later come to be understood as neoliberalism.[71] Arun Kundnani draws attention to how Powell had long been the most prominent advocate of neoliberalism, resigning as Financial Secretary in 1958 over the government's refusal to end increases in social spending. Throughout the 1960s, Powell made speeches criticising public ownership, economic planning and social spending and espousing what he termed the doctrine of the market.[72] As Robbie Shilliam puts it: 'Powell's political strategy was to dis-identify the Conservative Party with the corporatist state ... and race was the modality by which neoliberal subjectivity ... [would be] politically induced.'[73]

Further, for neoliberalism to succeed and capture the public imagination, it would have to persuade parts of the working class

> to be more loyal to the nation-state than it was to its own interests. As Powell's friend and admirer Peregrine Worsthorne wrote in 1970, if a Conservative government was 'going to re-activate the class war' by attempting to implement neoliberal policies, it would need a populist figure like Enoch Powell to secure a 'patriotic hold over working-class votes'.[74]

Racism became 'the means by which class was to be bound to the nation; the more that workers rallied around whiteness rather than class interests, the weaker they would be'.[75] Tragically, history demonstrates that Powell calculated correctly, that summoning a racializing conception of British nationalism built around a white identity would strike a chord with important sections of the working class. Demonstrations and strikes in support of Powell took place almost immediately, with the majority occurring in his home base of the West Midlands.[76] Construction and power station workers in Wolverhampton and Birmingham took industrial action followed by 'some twenty or so strikes, involving perhaps 10–12,000 workers, with the largest … involving … workers at Motor Panels in Coventry, the Dunlop tyre factory near Gateshead, and Smithfield meat market in London'.[77] There were also a number of workplaces where workers, including trade union representatives, circulated petitions supporting Powell's right to free speech and his opposition to further immigration.[78]

The climax of this wave of racist strikes occurred between 23 April and 26 April 1968, when London dockers struck in support of Powell. On the first day, 1,000 dockers from the West India Dock in Poplar came out on strike in protest against Powell's sacking. Some then marched from the East End to Westminster carrying placards reading 'Don't knock Enoch' and 'Back Britain, not Black Britain'.[79] The following day, 600 dockers at St Katherine's Docks in Wapping walked out in support of Powell while in nearby Deptford two wharves stopped work due to a strike involving 150 men. On Thursday 25 April, 500 men were absent from work at riverside wharves in the Upper and Lower Pools in Southwark and Bermondsey, and on Friday 26 April some 4,400 men stayed away from work in the largest sectors, the Royal group of docks in Newham.[80] Harry Pennington, leader of the strike at the Royal Docks, insisted he 'wanted a total ban on immigration because there were enough immigrants here already'.[81]

Another dockers' leader, Harry Pearman, headed a delegation that met with Powell in the House of Commons, after which he declared 'I have just met Enoch Powell and it made me feel proud to be an Englishman. He told me that he felt that if this matter was swept under the rug, he would lift the rug and do the same again. We are representatives of the working man.'[82] Overall, 'about a third of the registered labour force – between 6,000 and 7,000 men – were involved in strike action in the week'.[83] And amid this wave of industrial action, 600 meat porters from Smithfield market struck and marched to Westminster to hand Powell a 92-page petition supporting his speech. A Gallup poll carried out at the end of April 1968 showed that 74 per cent of the population agreed with Powell's speech, with only 15 per cent disagreeing.[84]

Powell had calculated that the scale of such racist mobilisations would force the political class to place the question of repatriation of black and brown Britons on the political agenda. However, he misjudged elite opinion. While there was a bipartisan consensus on the need for racist immigration controls, these elites also understood that one of the legacies of empire would be the creation of a settled population of black and brown Britons. This was commonly understood to be the opportunity cost of maintaining leadership of the Commonwealth – an important trading bloc as well as an institution through which to protect and maintain Britain's geopolitical interests. Consequently, and much to his chagrin, Powell found himself condemned by the political elites, including most of the Conservative leadership. Four of his shadow cabinet colleagues, McLeod, Boyle, Hogg and Carr, threatened to resign unless he was sacked. The leader of the Conservative Party, Heath, did just that the following day, arguing that his speech was 'inflammatory and liable to damage race relations'.[85]

Despite this censure, Powell's speech unleashed a wave of violent racism against Britain's settled Asian and Caribbean communities. Already confined to the bottom of the British class structure through racist working class and employer collusion, in those regions and localities where multi-ethnic working-class communities resided, a catastrophe unfolded.[86] In one incident in Tower Hamlets in the East End of London, more than 50 youths raced through the market smashing the windows of Pakistani-owned shops leaving three people requiring hospital treatment. The intensity of racist violence was such that Salman Ali – the Pakistani High Commissioner – was forced to intervene. In the immediate aftermath of more than 20 violent racist attacks, including the murder of Tosir Ali on 6 April 1970, he visited the East End of London 'to let the Pakistani community there know that he was very concerned about the attacks on them'. He also informed journalists that discussions had been held with the local Community Relations Council and that the matter 'would be put before the Home Office and the authorities concerned'.[87]

But such rhetoric did little to arrest the violence and discrimination. Racism became the lens through which concerns about class injustice were lived and fought over. The black and Asian working class found itself thoroughly dehumanised and brutalised. The reach of such racism was so deep that it extended into the everyday policing of racialized social norms in social settings, including intimate relations, suggesting racism was about more than economic matters. And to this must be added the still unregistered costs of living, or rather, surviving amid such durable and suffo-cating forms of oppression; not just the injuries arising from everyday discrimination but the heartache that individual men, women and children endured as they lived out damaged lives watching the calamities pile one on top of another. Through Powell, 'The English had begun to know themselves once more. In the obscene form of racism.'[88]

Ever since the defeat of Chartism in the 1840s, racism has proved to be the Achilles heel of the working class. Institutions established to advance the cause of social justice have simultaneously become self-actualising agents in the production of racialized difference, helping to reinforce the bifurcation of the working class through the consolidation of new hierarchies of labour. No romanticised accounts of a golden age of social democracy in the age of democratic capitalism can be sustained when this history is brought into view. Instead, our reading against the grain draws attention to the carnival of racist reaction that emanated from all social classes, undermining the hopes and desires of Asian and Caribbean workers to live a life of happiness and contentedness.

Notes

1 Tom Nairn, 'The Nature of the Labour Party (Part II)', *New Left Review* 1, no. 28 (1964): 35.
2 Satnam Virdee, 'Class, Racism and the Politics of Vacuum', in *Corbynism from Below*, edited by Mark Perryman (London: Lawrence & Wishart, 2019).
3 Tom Nairn, *The Break-Up of Britain: Crisis and Neo-Nationalism*, Third Edition (London: Verso Books, 2021).
4 Nairn, 'The Nature of the Labour Party (Part II)', 36.
5 James Vernon, 'The History of Britain Is Dead; Long Live a Global History of Britain', *History Australia* 13, no. 1 (2016): 32.
6 Cited in Gupta, *Imperialism and the British Labour Movement, 1914–1964*, 281.
7 Cited in Gupta, *Imperialism and the British Labour Movement, 1914–1964*, 305–6.

8 Cited in Nairn, 'The Nature of the Labour Party (Part II)', 38.
9 Bhambra, 'Relations of Extraction, Relations of Redistribution', 12.
10 Cited in Gupta, *Imperialism and the British Labour Movement, 1914–1964*, 320.
11 Alfie Hancox, 'Alfie Hancox: The Imperialist Soul of Social Democrats', *The Elephant* (blog), 16 July 2021, www.theelephant.info/ideas/2021/07/16/the-imperialist-soul-of-social-democrats/.
12 Allister Hinds, 'Sterling and Decolonization in the British Empire, 1945–1958', *Social and Economic Studies* 48, no. 4 (1999): 105.
13 Cited in Gupta, *Imperialism and the British Labour Movement, 1914–1964*, 324.
14 Hinds, 'Sterling and Decolonization in the British Empire, 1945–1958', 102.
15 Sir Stafford Cripps was an important exception, an anti-imperialist of a liberal persuasion.
16 Kathleen Paul, *Whitewashing Britain: Race and Citizenship in the Postwar Era* (Ithaca, NY: Cornell University Press, 1997), 119.
17 Robert Miles and Diana Kay, 'The TUC, Foreign Labour and the Labour Government, 1945–1951', *Immigrants & Minorities* 9, no. 1 (1990): 85–108.
18 John Solomos, *Race and Racism in Britain*, Third Edition (Basingstoke: Palgrave Macmillan, 2003), 49.
19 David Owen, 'Ethnic Minorities in Great Britain: Patterns of Population Change, 1981–91', Census Statistical Paper (Coventry: Centre for Research in Ethnic Relations, University of Warwick, 1995), 1.
20 Bob Carter, Clive Harris and Shirley Joshi, 'The 1951–55 Conservative Government and the Racialization of Black Immigration', *Immigrants & Minorities* 6, no. 3 (1 November 1987): 336.
21 Solomos, *Race and Racism in Britain*, 52. The growing demands for national citizenship in Canada and Australia, and the independence of India had forced the Labour government to clarify the terms of citizenship. Committed to remaining at the epicentre of a reconstituted imperial Commonwealth it passed the British Nationality Act of 1948 which effectively opened up citizenship to 850 million subjects.

22 Peter Hennessy, *The Prime Minister: The Office and its Holders Since 1945* (London: Penguin, 2001), 205.

23 Cited in Ian Hedworth John Little Gilmour, *Inside Right: A Study of Conservatism* (London: Hutchinson, 1977), 134.

24 Carter *et al.*, 'The 1951–55 Conservative Government and the Racialization of Black Immigration', 337.

25 Virdee, *Racism, Class and the Racialized Outsider*, 102–3.

26 Virdee, *Racism, Class and the Racialized Outsider*, 103.

27 Mark R. Duffield, *Black Radicalism and the Politics of Deindustrialization: The Hidden History of Indian Foundry Workers in the West Midlands* (Aldershot: Avebury, 1988), 3.

28 Nina Fishman, 'No Home but the Trade Union Movement', in *Opening the Books: Essays on the Social and Cultural History of British Communist Party*, edited by Geoff Andrews, Nina Fishman and Kevin Morgan (London: Pluto Press, 1995), 116.

29 Evan Smith, '"Class before Race": British Communism and the Place of Empire in Postwar Race Relations', *Science & Society* 72, no. 4 (2008): 457–58.

30 Smith, 'Class before Race', 458.

31 The important work of Jodi Burkett, however, has identified the emergence of leftist social movements in this period including the Campaign for Nuclear Disarmament and the Anti-Apartheid Movement that did force a more rigorous reckoning with questions of empire and racism. See Jodi Burkett, *Constructing Post-Imperial Britain: Britishness, 'Race' and the Radical Left in the 1960s* (Basingstoke: Palgrave Macmillan, 2013).

32 Virdee, *Racism, Class and the Racialized Outsider*; Priyamvada Gopal, *Insurgent Empire: Anticolonial Resistance and British Dissent* (London: Verso Books, 2020).

33 Gopal, *Insurgent Empire*, 4.

34 Marika Sherwood, *Claudia Jones: A Life in Exile*, First Edition (London: Lawrence & Wishart, 1999), 126.

35 Sherwood, *Claudia Jones*, 89–124.

36 Cited in Kevin Morgan, Gidon Cohen and Andrew Flinn, *Communists and British Society 1920–1991: People of a Special Mould* (London: Rivers Oram Press, 2005), 203.

37 Wm Roger Louis, *The Oxford History of the British Empire: Volume IV: The Twentieth Century*, edited by Judith Brown and Wm Roger Louis (Oxford: Oxford University Press, 1999), 343.

38 Louis, *The Oxford History of the British Empire*, 330.
39 Cited in Alan Travis, 'After 44 Years Secret Papers Reveal Truth about Five Nights of Violence in Notting Hill', *The Guardian*, 24 August 2002, www.theguardian.com/uk/2002/aug/24/artsan dhumanities.nottinghillcarnival2002.
40 B. Schwarz, '"The Only White Man in There": The Re-Racialisation of England, 1956–1968', *Race & Class* 38, no. 1 (1996): 65–78.
41 Gurminder K. Bhambra, 'Locating Brexit in the Pragmatics of Race, Citizenship and Empire', in *Brexit: Sociological Responses*, edited by William Outhwaite (London: Anthem Press, 2017), 91–99.
42 Cited in Solomos, *Race and Racism in Britain*, 56.
43 Tom Nairn, 'Labour Imperialism', *New Left Review* 1, no. 32 (1965): 6.
44 Importantly, long-term British decline since the Second World War is mostly an artefact of other countries being more successful. See David Edgerton, *The Rise and Fall of the British Nation: A Twentieth-Century History* (London: Penguin, 2019).
45 Entry would be ratified through a referendum conducted in 1975 when Labour had returned to power under Wilson.
46 Later, the EU social chapter was introduced but this was not a product of working class self-activity but delivered as an elite response to manage growing social inequalities.
47 Nairn, 'The Nature of the Labour Party (Part II)', 52.
48 Nairn, 'The Nature of the Labour Party (Part II)', 52–53.
49 Michael Moran, *The Politics of Industrial Relations* (London: Palgrave Macmillan, 1980).
50 Keith Grint, *The Sociology of Work: An Introduction* (Cambridge: Polity Press, 1991).
51 John E. Kelly, *Trade Unions and Socialist Politics* (London: Verso Books, 1988), 107.
52 Kelly, *Trade Unions and Socialist Politics*, 108–9.
53 Ralph Darlington, *The Dynamics of Workplace Unionism: Shop Stewards' Organization in Three Merseyside Plants*, First Edition (London: Thomson Learning, 1994).
54 Wolfgang Streeck, 'The Crises of Democratic Capitalism', *New Left Review* 1, no. 71 (2011): 5–29.
55 Kelly, *Trade Unions and Socialist Politics*, 109.

56 Johan Verberckmoes, 'The United Kingdom: Between Policy and Practice', in *The Lost Perspective? Trade Unions between Ideology and Social Action in the New Europe*, edited by Patrick Pasture, Johan Verberckmoes and Hans de Witte (Aldershot: Avebury, 1996), 227; Kelly, *Trade Unions and Socialist Politics*.

57 Smith, 'Class before Race'.

58 John McIlroy, *Trade Unions in Britain Today*, Second Edition (Manchester: Manchester University Press, 1995), 104.

59 Ian H. Birchall, *The Smallest Mass Party in the World: Building the Socialist Workers Party, 1951–1979* (London: Socialists Unlimited, 1981).

60 Nairn, 'Labour Imperialism'.

61 William Wentworth Daniel, *Racial Discrimination in England* (London: Penguin Books, 1968), 82.

62 Daniel, *Racial Discrimination in England*, 209.

63 Daniel, *Racial Discrimination in England*, 217.

64 Cited in Solomos, *Race and Racism in Britain*, 84. For an excellent discussion see Ian Sanjay Patel, *We're Here Because You Were There: Immigration and the End of Empire* (London: Verso Books, 2021), 209–42.

65 *The Times* said the legislation established a 'colour bar' and was 'probably the most shameful measure that the Labour members have ever been asked by their whip to support', cited in Solomos, *Race and Racism in Britain*, 60.

66 Camilla Schofield, *Enoch Powell and the Making of Postcolonial Britain* (Cambridge: Cambridge University Press, 2013).

67 Cited in Simon Heffer, *Like the Roman: The Life of Enoch Powell*, Second Edition (London: Weidenfield & Nicolson, 1998), 451.

68 Cited in Heffer, *Like the Roman*, 451.

69 Arun Kundnani, 'Disembowel Enoch Powell', *Dissent Magazine* (blog), 2018, www.dissentmagazine.org/online_articles/enoch-powell-racism-neoliberalism-right-wing-populism-rivers-of-blood; Nairn, 'Labour Imperialism', 6.

70 Tom Nairn, 'Enoch Powell: The New Right', *New Left Review* 1, no. 61 (1970): 5.

71 Robbie Shilliam, 'Enoch Powell: Britain's First Neoliberal Politician', *New Political Economy* 26, no. 2 (2021): 239–49;

Kundnani, 'Disembowel Enoch Powell'. According to Shilliam, 'Powellism clearly laid the ideational and electoral groundwork for Thatcherism.' Shilliam, 'Enoch Powell', 246.

72 Kundnani, 'Disembowel Enoch Powell'; Shilliam, 'Enoch Powell', 242–44.

73 Shilliam, 'Enoch Powell', 243, 246.

74 Kundnani, 'Disembowel Enoch Powell'.

75 Kundnani, 'Disembowel Enoch Powell'.

76 For further information about the ramifications of the speech in Wolverhampton itself, see Shirin Hirsch, *In the Shadow of Enoch Powell: Race, Locality and Resistance* (Manchester: Manchester University Press, 2018).

77 Fred Lindop, 'Racism and the Working Class: Strikes in Support of Enoch Powell in 1968', *Labour History Review* 66, no. 1 (2001): 79–100.

78 Lindop, 'Racism and the Working Class', 82.

79 Heffer, *Like the Roman*, 462.

80 Lindop, 'Racism and the Working Class', 82.

81 Cited in Lindop, 'Racism and the Working Class', 84.

82 Cited in Andrew Roth, *Enoch Powell: Tory Tribune* (London: TBS The Book Service Ltd, 1970), 360.

83 Lindop, 'Racism and the Working Class', 82.

84 Heffer, *Like the Roman*, 467.

85 Heffer, *Like the Roman*, 461.

86 Stephen Ashe, Satnam Virdee and Laurence Brown, 'Striking Back against Racist Violence in the East End of London, 1968–1970', *Race & Class* 58, no. 1 (2016): 34–54.

87 Ashe *et al.*, 'Striking Back against Racist Violence', 43.

88 Nairn, 'Enoch Powell', 13.

3 Anti-racism, socialist utopias and neoliberal reaction

In the course of the 1970s, Britain's relative economic decline mutated into a full-blown crisis of hegemony. Since the end of the Second World War, ruling elites had undertaken multifarious efforts to resolve the crisis brought on by the end of empire. By the 1970s, that crisis now spilled over into the political and cultural domains, thoroughly destabilising capitalist rule. Unprecedented fissures as well as unexpected solidarities would become distinctive features of this period, as men and women from all backgrounds were thrust into the struggle over the future direction of society. This chapter documents the new utopian projects of socialist transformation that emerged, and the infrastructures and ideas that animated them. At times, these projects moved well beyond the logic of Labourism to realise the desire of oppressed and exploited people of all colours to live a life of happiness and contentedness. It also maps the simultaneous break from the neoliberal right initiated by Powell and realised by Margaret Thatcher in her capture of the Conservative Party leadership. Her subsequent General Election victory in May 1979 would launch the most concerted attack on the organised working class since the 1920s, undermining the organisational infrastructure that sustained the politics and language of class and socialism. By recovering this hidden history in its complex and contradictory totality, this chapter shows that the transformation of Britain from a Fordist to a more flexible model of accumulation that we now understand as neoliberalism was not inevitable. Rather, it was dependent upon extinguishing a counter-hegemonic project that crystallised in the form of an emergent multi-ethnic politics of class. This is why we understand neoliberalism as a capitalist counter-revolution.

How Asians and Caribbeans became black[1]

The response of the organised labour movement to the wave of racist strikes and violence that followed Powell's incendiary 'rivers of blood' speech in 1968 ranged from the indifferent to the hostile. Anti-racist socialist David Widgery recounted:

> We were just completely shocked numb ... You suddenly realised how little influence the Left really had, how the roots of political organisations like the Communist Party had been rotting in the soil ... Just how urgent things had become ... I seemed to spend the next few days leafleting solidly and I'll never forget the look on the faces of the Pakistani postmen when they read the leaflets and found out they weren't fascist. For those few days after Powell, they were petrified. But so was I.[2]

In the absence of working-class solidarity and the Labour Party's unwillingness to consistently champion the cause of racial justice, Caribbean and Asian activists began forging their own oppositional cultures of solidarity.[3] Existing welfare organisations, such as the Indian Workers' Association (IWA), the West Indian Standing Conference and the Pakistani Workers Association were repurposed to fight racism. As Avtar Jouhl, a socialist in the Birmingham IWA, put it:

> We feel that we are an integral part of the British working class while we are here. While we are employed here, we are part and parcel of the British working class. It is another thing that the British working class may not think so. It is not the

sincerity, the willingness, the class position of the Indian and
the black workers which is on trial. It is the internationalism
of the British working class which is on trial.[4]

Many of these activists drew their inspiration from the
struggles waged against decolonisation across Asia, Africa
and the Caribbean. Reframing the struggle against racism
in Britain as a transnational movement against imperialism
and socialism, activists like Jouhl spoke not only of opposing
the 'colour bar' but of 'promoting socialism, peace and
friendship, workers unity, colonial freedom'.[5] Opposition to
imperialism and advocacy of international working-class solidarity were consistent motifs of the IWA:

> Here in Birmingham, we take pride of place in this pageant
> of International Brotherhood. Despite differences in countries
> of origin, in colour or the languages that we speak, we march
> arm in arm sharing a common hand, for we are all workers.
> The [IWA] extends brotherly greetings to the workers of
> Birmingham and pledges itself to the cause of working class
> unity and peace. We also send greetings to our brethren in
> distant lands fighting against imperialism – to our brethren in
> Cuba, in Laos and throughout Africa.[6]

Also, influential in shaping the outlook of Asian and
Caribbean activists was the struggle for civil rights being
waged by African Americans in the United States. In late 1964
and early 1965, the leaders of the two wings of the American
racial justice movement – Martin Luther King and Malcolm
X – visited Britain. King stopped off in London en route to
Stockholm, where he was scheduled to receive the Nobel
Peace Prize. Drawing inspiration from his visit, migrant
groups representing Caribbean, Pakistani and Indian communities came together with white anti-racists to establish the
Campaign Against Racial Discrimination (CARD) in January
1965. More influential proved to be Malcolm X's visits in
late 1964 and again in February 1965, just days before his

assassination in Harlem, New York City. In important talks delivered at the Oxford Union and the London School of Economics, he outlined his internationalist vision of a global struggle of subjugated peoples, of the 'exploited against the exploiter' where 'the same pulse that beats in the Black man on the African continent today is beating in the heart of the Black man in North America, Central America, South America, and in the Caribbean'.[7]

Significantly, at the invitation of Avtar Jouhl he also visited Smethwick, the small town near Birmingham, which had been witness to a vicious racist campaign less than a year earlier. At the gathering, Malcolm X encouraged black and Asian people to organise autonomously to combat such racism. Alongside these existing organisations, new umbrella formations were established. On Sunday 28 April 1968, the day that dockers and porters marched in support of Powell, representatives from more than 20 minority organisations came together in Leamington Spa, West Midlands, to form the Black People's Alliance (BPA). Purposively formed to unite 'black people against racialism and imperialism' and to 'seek allies from the majority community', its elected convenor, Jagmohan Joshi, informed *The Birmingham Post* that 'black people have decided to go for militant action … When guerrilla strikes take place and dockers march in favour of a racialist, the situation is grim … We feel that the time has come when we ought to defend ourselves and our families.'[8]

He continued: 'Let those who talk of "freedom of expression" for racists understand that we too want freedom to live our lives unmolested.' The BPA deployed a variety of strategies, from mobilising the Caribbean and Asian unemployed to organising workers in a range of industrial settings, including transport, health care, schools, factories and offices.[9] In December 1968, a Black Youth Conference organised by the BPA at Birmingham Town Hall was attended by over 2,000 activists from London, Sheffield, Nottingham, Bradford and Manchester, as well as several towns in the midlands. The conference heard speeches from Tariq Ali (International Marxist Group), Roy Sawh (Universal Coloured People's Association), Gerry Archer (West Indian People's Union) and Mihr Gupta (Indian Association and the Birmingham Advisory Council for Commonwealth Immigrants).[10] While speakers were agreed on the importance of uniting 'immigrant organisations' to fight racism, Gupta called for the conference to 'pledge ourselves to the philosophy which will unite us – the philosophy of Black Power'.[11]

As the BPA turned to the 'politics of the street', their anti-imperialist activities included a 500-strong demonstration at Rhodesia House in London in 1969, with demonstrators clashing with both the police and National Front supporters in Charing Cross.[12] During the protest, two demonstrators climbed to the top of the building to remove the Rhodesian flag. Protestors marched to Downing Street flanked by several organisations, including the Zimbabwe Solidarity Committee, the Universal Coloured People's Association (UCPA), the Vietnam Solidarity Campaign and the Revolutionary Student Socialist Federation. Slogans at the march included 'Enoch Powell Out, Wilson Out, Racialism Out', 'Disembowel Powell' and 'Police brutality on the increase since Powell's speech'.[13] Once there, they submitted a petition stating 'We must put up a united front. Only when we are in a position of strength based on pride and confidence will white people talk to us.'[14]

The BPA's attempts to connect the struggle against racism in Britain to wider demands for colonial liberation abroad was also evident in January 1969, when they wrote to the heads of state of Commonwealth countries asking to raise the issue of racial justice at their forthcoming conference in London.[15] The BPA and the IWA-GB organised coaches to bring demonstrators from Birmingham, Manchester, Bradford and Leeds to participate in a 'march of dignity' and to 'show the Prime Ministers from the Commonwealth that Britain had failed to solve her race problems'.[16]

Fifty-five organisations affiliated to the BPA within the first year of its existence, including the IWA, UCPA and the Black

Unity and Freedom Party. What was striking about the BPA as well as other organisations of the time was the solidarity that was forged in struggle between activists and populations from Caribbean, Indian and Pakistani backgrounds. While the racisms facing these communities often differed in form and content, what defined this emergent social movement was the shared desire among activists to forge a multi-ethnic coalition of the racialized poor that would not only mobilise against escalating state and street racisms, but for class politics and socialist transformation.

Further, these activists sought to stretch the category of class to encompass Asian and Caribbean workers. In this sense, black self-organisation was a mechanism by which they attempted to both challenge racism and, in the process, make white workers aware of the importance of class solidarity across racialized groups. Significantly, this socialism was more internationalist in content than prevailing British variants. The idea of the nation didn't constrain their imaginary; after all, it was the entanglement of socialism with British nationalism that was responsible for enforcing their second-class status. Instead, their socialism was stretched to encompass anti-imperialist, Marxist and black power influences (and eventually feminism). In the process, it re-imagined the struggle in Britain as an integral part of the then still unfolding quest for colonial freedom, justice and human dignity for the darker peoples of the world. Organisations such as the Universal Coloured People's Association and the Black Unity and Freedom Party helped cement this Caribbean–Asian unity.[17] Further, through the Organisation of Women of African and Asian Descent, women of colour developed an innovative socialist-feminist strategy to challenge sexism as well as racism.[18]

Such Asian–Caribbean solidarity was also reflected in the plethora of newspapers and journals that sprang up in this period, such as *Race Today*, *Black Liberator* and *Race and Class*. The intensity of the activity in this period is neatly captured by Kalbir Shukra:

The 'black' radical activist was usually an unpaid campaigner who operated intensively with a small group of like-minded people, went from meeting to meeting, distributed pamphlets, spoke at rallies, carried banners and organised demonstrations to convince what was termed 'West Indian', 'Indian' and 'Pakistani' people that their experience of inferior treatment at the hands of employers, schools, local authorities, government officials, politicians and the police was unacceptable. Crucially, they also argued that this situation could be changed through militant political activity, primarily against employers and the state ... the black activists used the term 'black' to build a movement to mobilise and cohere self-reliant communities of resistance to racism.[19]

By the early 1970s, then, a powerful organisational infra-structure had been established through the increasingly entangled activities of Asian and Caribbean activists united by their commitment to a socialist anti-racist politics. Through marches and demonstrations, workplace strikes and legal campaigns, these disparate groups had come together around the identification of black. That is, regardless of whether they happened to be of Caribbean, Indian or Pakistani descent, the imposed and stigmatised identity of 'black' was appropriated and infused with a new meaning out of which emerged 'communities of resistance'.[20] As Sivanandan put it, 'black was the colour of our fight, our politics, not our skin'.[21]

These struggles of race and class emerged from a funda-mental contradiction between a suffocating racism that denied black and Asian workers their humanity and the desires of those same people to live a contented life of happiness and completeness. This variance between lack and longing enabled activists to relativise the present and prise open the possibility that the suffering of today was neither natural nor given, and that an alternative, more hopeful future was possible. And it was this desire to not just imagine an alternative future but to will it into existence by giving history a nudge that gave this movement its utopian and emancipatory force.[22]

The formation of a multi-ethnic politics of class
through the detour of race

When we place this wave of black insurgency alongside the
class struggles described in the previous chapter, growing
student unrest, the struggle for women's liberation and the
emergence of the Civil Rights Movement in Northern Ireland,
the depth of the legitimation crisis facing the British state
becomes more transparent.[23] With the financial cushion of
empire no longer available and Caribbean and Asian workers
collectively opposing their super-exploitation, there was little
left in the armoury of the British elites to assuage this wave
of domestic conflicts. Traditional mechanisms such as racist
nationalism that had formed such an essential component
of consensual rule in Britain over the previous century were
now being challenged by a minority. It is in this moment,
in the early 1970s, that a distinctive shift can be discerned
towards what the Marxist philosopher Nicos Poulantzas
called 'authoritarian statism'. In such crises of capitalism,
political features that are thought of as exceptional become
normalised. In Poulantzas' words, this conjuncture comes
to be defined by 'intensified state control over every sphere
of socio-economic life [which] is combined with the radical
decline of the institutions of political democracy and with
draconian and multiform curtailment of so-called "formal"
liberties'.[24] Britain in 1971 was one such moment. It was an
inflection point which saw not only the implementation of the
Industrial Relations Act but internment and mass arrests in
Northern Ireland, and the passing of an immigration act that
effectively removed the right of Caribbean and Asian people
to settle in Britain on the grounds they were not patrials.[25]

Further, this shift towards a repressive 'law and order
society' was mediated through fresh ideological work. In
particular, new moral panics and accompanying folk-devils
were amplified to win the consent of 'the silent majority' for
this increasingly coercive use of state power.[26] The aim was to
restore social order necessary to facilitate the accumulation

of capital. The reproduction of racism, detached from a lost empire, increasingly focused on black and brown Britons. The twin concerns of uncontrolled immigration and the problems arising from it would be emphasised again and again.[27] This racializing state strategy not only infected the two main political parties, but legitimated the arguments of the National Front, which saw its vote rise from scarcely 12,000 at the 1970 General Election to 77,000 in February 1974, before almost doubling again to 114,000 votes in the October 1974 election.[28] Significantly, events like the Imperial Typewriters strike in Leicester in 1974 demonstrated the capacity of the National Front to draw support from the less well-organised sections of the manual white working class residing in ethnically mixed areas of residential settlement.

At the same time, the emancipatory movements engaged in collective motion would not be easily subdued. The uplifting visions of freedom and human dignity painted by Asian and Caribbean struggles for racial justice had rehumanised black and brown workers. Further, many of the white socialist activists leading the class struggles of the 1970s were now more alive to the dangers of racism and how it undermined their advocacy of collective action and working-class solidarity. Through the existence of shared political networks, they understood first-hand that self-organisation by black and Asian activists never implied any sort of permanent separation from white workers, but instead was intended to open their eyes to the depth of the problem. As Avtar Jouhl, General Secretary of the Birmingham IWA, explained: 'We feel unity will develop in struggle. This does not in any sense deny the need for black workers to have their own caucuses in every factory and place of work. We do not advocate separate black unions; that would be to play the capitalists' game of dividing the working class.'[29]

As the century-old democratic settlement was disintegrating, working-class attachment to dominant racialized conceptions of the British nation were being loosened. That is, between a collapsing welfare state settlement and an emergent neoliberalism whose victory was not yet assured, the moral worth of black and Asian workers underwent a process of mental recalibration such that some white workers who had either been indifferent or even racist were now willing to engage in solidarity action. In this moment, it became possible to imagine a politics of class that didn't require denying someone's humanity but insisted on justice for all.

Socialists used their newly acquired authority to begin shifting the unwieldy bureaucratic tanker that was the British labour movement towards anti-racism. This did not happen overnight but took several years of intense political activity. The first indications could be discerned by the early 1970s with the increase in the volume of speeches and motions tabled at large trade union conferences that called on the labour movement to take active steps to combat racism. And at the 1973 TUC annual conference, socialists were successful in moving a motion which called upon the next Labour government to repeal the racist 1971 Immigration Act, thereby reversing the decision taken at the same conference two years previously.[30]

Over and over, socialists explained to its growing publics how the organised labour movement had underestimated the depth of racist sentiment within the British working class, and that steps needed to be urgently taken to combat it. A pamphlet released by a rank and file docker and formally endorsed with a foreword by Jack Jones – then leader of the TGWU – declared: 'The harsh reality is that the working class is divided by racialism to a damaging degree. An urgent responsibility falls upon trade union activists to seek those remedies which can unify our class and meet head-on the racialism embedded in so much of our society.'[31]

What is striking about this passage is the discursive reframing of Caribbean and Asian workers from 'immigrants' to members of 'our' class. It indicated an effort to stretch the language of the labour movement to accommodate the ethnic diversity of the working class in Britain. At its 1974 annual conference, the TUC acknowledged for the first time in its 110-year history that black workers were subject to racism and discriminatory practice. Further, it called on trade unions to 'actively oppose racialism within their own ranks' as well as the organised far right.[32] At the following year's conference, delegates from several affiliated unions made speeches denouncing the racism of the National Front and called upon members to expose the threat of fascist racism to working-class solidarity.

Local trades councils also increasingly mobilised against the National Front through the formation of anti-racist and anti-fascist committees. An organisational infrastructure to tackle racism was put in place including the establishment of the TUC's Race Relations Advisory Committee. Against this combined pressure from black movements and white socialists, the Labour government was pressed to make good on its manifesto promise of tackling racism. It did so by introducing the 1976 Race Relations Act. The legislation was pathbreaking in so far as it made acts of indirect as well as direct discrimination illegal.[33]

'The workers united will never be defeated': the Grunwick strike

The culmination of this movement towards the formation of a multi-ethnic politics of class came during the Grunwick strike. In August 1976, a handful of mainly Asian women led by Jayaben Desai took strike action against the brutal management practices in a photographic print facility in north-west London. Employing around 440 workers, the Grunwick factory was renowned for its harsh conditions, including arbitrary threats of dismissal for refusing to increase output, compulsory overtime and persistent racist and sexist harassment. The strikers joined the Association of Professional, Executive and Computer Staff (APEX) who immediately made the dispute official, putting the workers on strike pay. Grunwick's management responded to the unionisation drive by dismissing the strikers, to which Desai defiantly responded: 'If you refuse to talk to us, we will turn off all the taps, one by one, until you have to.'[34]

At the 1976 TUC annual conference, Roy Grantham, General Secretary of APEX, called for wider trade union support for the strikers, drawing attention directly to how racism was central to their exploitation. Tom Jackson of the Union of Post Office Workers promised to block the delivery of mail coming in or out of Grunwick, effectively preventing the business from operating. Solidarity action also flowed from hundreds of local workers who donated money and food and joined the picket line. The management's refusal to concede to the strikers' demands forced the strike committee to call for a mass picket of the firm. On 13 June 1977 – ten months on from the start of the dispute – mass picketing began with around 3,000 people, including miners from the coalfields of South Wales, Scotland and Yorkshire. Meanwhile, post office staff continued to prevent the delivery of mail, and contracted TGWU drivers refused to drive the police onto the firm's premises. This solidarity action transformed the dispute into one of national significance. The largest picket occurred on 11 July 1977, when an estimated 18,000 workers, socialists, anti-racists and feminists joined Desai and the strikers in an unprecedented show of solidarity.

The mass picketing continued for a further five months until November 1977, when the Labour government exerted pressure on the trade union leaders to seek a negotiated settlement. In the same month, some of the Grunwick strikers went on hunger strike outside the TUC headquarters, demanding more effective support. APEX responded by suspending the hunger strikes and taking away their strike pay. The local postal workers who had prevented delivery of the mail to Grunwick were sacked. On 14 July 1978, with the trade union bureaucracy and the Labour Party leadership reasserting its control over the dispute, the strike was abandoned without any of the strikers' demands having been met.[35]

The Grunwick strike was a formative moment in British working-class history. Though defeated, it indicated that a transformation in political consciousness was taking place among important sectors of the organised working class. Having been previously attached to a narrow, sectionalist understanding of class informed by a racialized British nationalism, key groups of workers were now moving towards a more inclusive class politics that could encompass those of Caribbean and Asian descent. This was most powerfully exemplified in the solidarity action of the London dockers at Grunwick. While in 1968 many had marched in support of Powell, a decade later some of those same workers now marched with the Royal Docks Shop Stewards' banner at the head of a mass picket in support of the Asian strikers at Grunwick.[36]

It is difficult to imagine how this more expansive vision of class could have been generated without the prior existence of the socialist project of political blackness. Its significance was two-fold. First, it provided a pathway through which black and Asian people could collectively organise against the racism that scarred their lives. Second, it signalled to white socialists the importance of stretching the language and politics of class to accommodate questions of racism and anti-racism. In a period that had hitherto been defined by white worker indifference to such racism, this marked a significant transformation in the history of the British working class. What looked like a more universalist politics had in fact emerged from particularist pathways. That is, a multi-ethnic politics of class was achieved not by avoiding discussion about racism but having a reckoning with it. In this sense, this movement was not an imitation of an older politics that tended to reduce race to class, but rather, emerged out of an expansive particularism that wilfully entangled anti-racism with the politics of class. Such solidarity was never easy to construct. Conflicts and disagreement were rife because of the different ways in which diverse subaltern groups had been hierarchically positioned.[37] But the direction of travel pointed towards the construction of a mesh-like infrastructure of dissent made up of multiple counter-hegemonic movements.

It is important to caution, however, that the structural and symbolic force of racism in Britain was not waning. Instead, what we are drawing attention to are processes that are too often glossed over in race-blind as well as postcolonial histories of this period,[38] namely, the emergence of unprecedented solidarity across distinctive class and anti-racist movements. The white British population was bifurcating in its standpoint on racism, with some now willing to mobilise against it. This is why anti-racist class politics began to extend well beyond the workplace, with culture becoming a key site of political struggle. In the aftermath of a series of racist statements made by the musician Eric Clapton, Rock Against Racism (RAR) was established in 1976. In this moment of heightened racist and anti-racist politics, it harnessed 'the energy of new sounds like punk and reggae' to build an anti-racist social movement led by working-class youth.[39] RAR's intentions were crystallised in the first issue of its fanzine, *Temporary Hoarding*, in which it declared: 'We want Rebel music, street music. Music that breaks down people's fear of one another. Crisis music. Now music. Music that knows who the real enemy is. Rock Against Racism. Love Music Hate Racism.'[40]

And in November 1977, the Anti-Nazi League (ANL) was founded to counter the rising threat of the National Front which had recently secured 44,000 votes in Leicester and more than 119,000 votes in the London County elections. It organised in local estates and workplaces and coordinated demonstrations against the fascists. In doing so it presented its vision of the alternative society – one based on love, not hate; multi-ethnic solidarity, not racism. The large events that ANL/RAR organised throughout 1977 and 1978 brought together tens of thousands of individuals and emboldened many to challenge racism when they returned to their localities. A plethora of local groups flourished, including Students Against the Nazis, Teachers Against the Nazis, School Kids Against the Nazis, Skateboarders Against the Nazis and Football Fans Against the Nazis – all with the aim of actively challenging racist ideas and movements across the country.[41]

Why do we draw attention to these fissures and solidarities in the 1970s? Too often, accounts of the rise of neoliberalism present a story of seamless transition from Fordist to flexible regimes of accumulation.[42] What such histories fail to identify, however, is that there existed a two-decade interregnum defined by systematic and intensifying multi-level conflict. This is why we argue that neoliberalism was not inevitable. In these years of strife, not only Thatcherism but new projects of working-class justice for all were birthed. Just as the democratic settlement was being reversed, there were attempts to protect it, and not only that, there were also efforts to will into existence a new way of living, one that would finally reckon with the material and symbolic legacies of racism.

These mobilisations indicated that diverse left publics from trade unionists to racialized minorities and young people had shifted well beyond the political logic of Labourism. While the socialist left became far more prominent in the Labour Party, with Tony Benn coming within 1 per cent of displacing Dennis Healey as deputy leader in September 1981, almost a decade of intensifying collective action ultimately failed to remake the Labour Party as a vehicle for socialist transformation. And by then, the Conservative Party led by the neoliberal Margaret Thatcher were already in power.

Neoliberalism as capitalist counter-revolution

In 1975, Margaret Thatcher captured the Tory Party leadership. She filled her shadow cabinet with free-marketeers like Keith Joseph, Geoffrey Howe and John Biffen to serve alongside the still dominant 'wets' like Francis Pym, William Prior and William Whitelaw, who remained committed to the democratic settlement. This neoliberal right made considerable headway among Conservative constituencies by linking the 'principles of a free market with more congenial Conservative emphases on a stronger state in the fields of defence, law and order, and a strengthened family'.[43] This drift towards a more neoliberal form of state rule was mediated by what Stuart Hall called an authoritarian populism,[44] which condensed 'a wide range of popular discontents with the post-war economic and political order and mobilized them around an authoritarian, right-wing solution to the intensifying economic and political crisis in Britain. It signified a convergence between the demands of those in authority and the pleas of the populace to solve these crises.'[45]

Thatcher, in particular, displayed a remarkable capacity to

> translate the themes of the new economic liberalism into slogans and ideas that tapped popular discontent with many aspects of the existing state, such as the arbitrariness of bureaucracy, the inefficiency of nationalised industry, the burden of taxation, the 'privileges' enjoyed by immigrants, the damage caused by strikes, the lawlessness of demonstrations and the undermining of the independence and moral responsibility of families.[46]

Key to the translation, as Andrew Gamble points out, 'was the posing of central questions of government policy as problems of individual responsibility and individual choice. This ideology of self-help preached the right to be unequal, the need for self-reliance, and the need for everyone to take full responsibility for themselves and their families.'[47] By 'presenting itself as the radical force that was going to change things', the 'Right was able to sufficiently identify itself as a kind of populist political force, able to connect its message with the discontents people were experiencing under Labour'.[48]

The Conservative victory at the 1979 General Election was interpreted as a mandate to arrest capitalist decline by reversing the democratic settlement. The most pressing requirement was to break the power of organised labour,

which was viewed as the primary source of economic inef-
ficiency and the main obstacle to the operation of the free
market economy. The Ridley plan, formulated while the
Conservatives were still in opposition in 1977, proposed a
series of carefully orchestrated confrontations, beginning
with industries where workers were less well-organised,
leaving the most powerful groups such as the miners and
dockers until last.[49] In a series of bitter, drawn-out disputes,
the plan was successfully executed beginning with the defeat
of the steel workers and car workers. By 1981, a distinctive
pattern was unfolding that would increasingly define the
character of industrial relations throughout the 1980s. On
the one hand there was rank and file anger at the new man-
agerial practices provoking explosive bouts of strike action
that would fail to generate the necessary solidarity action
from workers in other industries. On the other, there was a
vacillating trade union leadership split between those who
were unable to face up to the changed relations of force –
characterised by an increasingly aggressive employing class,
and an unsympathetic government – and others, who
wished to negotiate and accommodate to these changes.
And accompanying this was 'the systematic removal of
collective and individual employment rights and the imposition of restrictions on various forms of unionised political
activity'.[50]

Alongside this, the increased emphasis on strict monet-
arist measures to control the rate of inflation went hand in
hand with a major programme of public spending cuts and
privatisation of state-held assets. These policies would contribute to the recession of 1979–81, when unemployment
doubled from 1.14 million (4.7 per cent of the labour force)
in June 1979 to 2.3 million (9.4 per cent) in June 1981.[51]
Manufacturing employment was particularly impacted,
with a quarter of all jobs lost between 1979 and 1983.[52]
The government's approach represented a wholesale rejec-
tion of the bipartisan commitment to full employment that
undergirded the ability of the organised working class to

play an active role in democratic deliberation in the work-place and beyond. It was tearing up the settlement that had taken a century to build.

The process of deindustrialisation, and the resulting loss of manufacturing jobs, had distinctively racialized class effects. The recession impacted disproportionately on Caribbean and Asian workers, with Caribbean youth, in particular, finding themselves unable to secure alternative employment due to the widespread operation of racist discriminatory practices. Intolerable levels of unemployment combined with systematic harassment by the police created a tipping point. In April 1981, in Brixton, South London, a riot broke out a week after the local police launched Swamp 81 – an oper-ation designed to combat an alleged increase in muggings and street crime.[53] The police had focused their attention overwhelmingly on black youth who accused them of treating 'us like dirt'. Such state racism also emboldened the National Front, as the events in Southall in July 1981 testify. Coachloads of fascist skinheads gathered at the Hambrough Tavern shouting racist abuse and attacking Asian residents. Hundreds of Asian youths responded by besieging the pub, setting it ablaze. These events were quickly followed by riots in over 30 towns and cities throughout July 1981, reflecting a wider sense of anger and despair that existed within black, Asian and white working-class communities under threat of destruction by the neoliberal Thatcherite juggernaut. By the end of the summer of 1981, more than 3,000 people had been arrested.[54]

While such continuing resistance draws attention to how contentious the policies of the Conservative administration were during the first half of the 1980s, it was also clear that Thatcher had cohered a cross-class coalition that was determined to see the defeat of organised labour and the emancipatory movements. And she understood, better than most, that racism was a potent mechanism to cohere the different fractions of classes as part of their wider effort to restore social order and re-secure the conditions for class domination. In fact, Thatcher had already signalled her intent in 1978 when she claimed:

> I think people are really rather afraid that this country might be rather swamped by people with a different culture and ... the British character has done so much for democracy and law, and has done so much throughout the world, that if there is any fear that it might be swamped, people are going to be really rather hostile to those coming in.[55]

This commentary was directed at former right-wing Tory voters and activists who had either retreated into political abstentionism under Heath or had joined the National Front in disgust at his censure of Powell. Thatcher's speech was an invitation to return home to their natural party of affiliation because the house had been put back in order. And she would follow this up by introducing the 1981 Nationality Act, which effectively stopped any further migration from the Caribbean and the Indian sub-continent.[56] Or, as one of her ministers, Timothy Raison contended, it would finally 'dispose of the lingering notion [that Britain] is somehow a haven for all whose countries we once ruled'.[57]

At the same time, Thatcher was not Powell. She and the neoliberals around her understood that the socialist anti-racist politics of the 1970s had rehumanised black and brown Britons. White Britons had bifurcated on the question of racism and repatriation was no longer a viable political option.[58] Therefore, an intrinsic component of their ideological renovation of authoritarian populism was to distance themselves from the fascists while at the same re-inscribing racism afresh through nationalism. This was reflected powerfully during the 1983 General Election, where a poster of a young man of Caribbean descent dressed in a suit was underscored by the strapline 'Labour says he's black, we say he's British.' It signalled to the wider population that black and brown Britons were here to stay, particularly if they assimilated and lived by the dominant cultural norms.

Meanwhile, the socialist anti-racism and black radicalism that had helped transform white British opinion in the first place was now strictly beyond the pale. Militant anti-racists joined Thatcher's growing pantheon of infamy, those 'enemies within' like socialists, feminists, trade unionists and other 'social deviants' that neoliberalism needed to defeat to re-secure social order and restore capitalist rule. The effects of this policy over time would prove to be striking. It bifurcated the different racialized communities with the culturally conservative and business-minded stratum securing a greater voice in public life, while at the same time, the socialist currents were repressed. Political blackness – a project that had united those of Caribbean and Asian descent – now fragmented and broke apart, to be replaced by increasingly distinctive modes of ethnicised and religious politics.[59] And these narrower forms of politics could be pursued not only through the Labour Party but increasingly the Conservative Party. This was just one of the ways in which the neoliberalism that drew its initial inspiration from Powell was modified and refashioned to partially encompass black and brown Britons. Through this, the Conservatives were able to further strengthen and incrementally expand their publics over the course of the 1980s and 1990s. Without these initial transformations in the late twentieth century, it is difficult to imagine how three of the four highest offices of state in early 2023 could be held by Conservatives of British Asian and Caribbean descent – Rishi Sunak (Prime Minister), Suella Braverman (Home Secretary) and James Cleverly (Foreign Secretary).

New fragmentations amid the decomposition of class

While never universally popular, this consistent attentiveness to the ideological and discursive registers of political life allowed Thatcherism to ultimately win the strategic engagements and defeat the left in all its multifarious forms. This would have a devastating impact on the collective psyche of the working class in Britain. By the late 1980s, a decade of unrelenting defeats at work and beyond had decisively weakened organised labour and the social movements. From now on, workers would become far less confident about taking collective action. The cycle of protest that began in the late 1960s encompassing a plethora of social and political struggles subsided. The employing class, ably supported by the Conservative government, began to carry through a decisive shift in the balance of class forces not seen since the defeat of the General Strike in the 1920s.

The traditional explanation for the ascendency of neoliberalism presents a story of a shift from a Fordist to a flexible regime of accumulation. However, such an account must be supplemented by the more expansive understanding that we have advanced here. Above all, it could not have been secured without extinguishing the educated hope produced by a two-decade cycle of sustained protest. Deep cracks had started to appear in the system of domination because different parts of the working class were envisioning alternative futures that relied on solidarity and opposition to entrenched social divisions. Such movements presented a concretised, albeit fragmentary, picture of an alternative to capitalism; a route out of a global system whose very survival is dependent on the maintenance of misery for the majority. That is why we believe the Thatcherite project of neoliberalism should be understood as capitalist counter-revolution – its ascendency measured by the shattered dreams and broken bodies of working-class populations all over Britain.[60] And over time, the vacuum created by the catastrophic defeat of the politics of educated hope would come to be filled by new modes of ideological classification and stigmatisation that would eventually restore the sense of hierarchical difference so essential to capitalist modernity's survival.

The 1980s, then, marked the opening moment in our still unfolding journey towards de-democratisation and the reversal of the settlement that had held firm for a century. The loss of empire had already eroded the economic basis of the inter-class truce. Now, the working class was denied the right to express its voice collectively in the neoliberal institutional arrangements of the British state. The different foundational pillars that secured the terms of the democratic settlement were beginning to unravel at pace. It is in this moment of catastrophic defeat of the multi-national and multi-ethnic working-class subject that we can discern the opening manifestations of the sorts of national fragmentations that define British politics today, including both Scottish independence and Brexit.

In England, the technical decomposition of class was accompanied by its political decomposition, as measured by the defeat of once powerful cultures of solidarity and socialist infrastructure built up over the course of the twentieth century. Such transformations destroyed the spirit and combativity of large sections of the multi-ethnic working class. Further, the socialist language of class declined, replaced by a sense of class disassociation, and later disidentification. In contrast, in Scotland, the effect of deindustrialisation was not to dissipate class consciousness but actually to strengthen it at first, with the Labour Party consolidating its hold north of the border. At the 1979 General Election, Labour won twice as many seats in Scotland as the Conservatives (44 to 22), and by 1987 they held five times as many (50 to 10).

While this was not reflected in the allocation of General Election seats, around one in seven voters were also breaking away from the two main parties to vote for alternatives, including, most importantly, the SNP. Narratives began to emerge that the Conservatives lacked a democratic mandate to carry out their policies in Scotland. William McIlvanney, in a celebrated lecture to the SNP annual conference in 1987 entitled 'Stands Scotland Where It Did?', argued that Thatcher was out to 'destroy' Scotland as a nation and its values:

> Margaret Thatcher is not just a perpetrator of bad policies. She is a cultural vandal. She takes the axe of her own simplicity to the complexities of Scottish life. She has no understanding of the hard-earned traditions she is destroying. And if we allow

her to continue, she will remove from the word 'Scottish' any meaning other than geographical ... We have never, in my lifetime, until now had a government whose basic principles were so utterly against the most essential traditions and aspirations of Scottish life ... I know nowhere less defined by materialism than Scotland.[61]

While the Conservative Party led by Thatcher never won the popular vote in Scotland, it was not because of her dislike of Scotland as the nationalists claimed. One only needs to consider the destruction wreaked across parts of England from the north-west to the south-east to grasp that the primary motivation of the Conservatives was to defeat the power of organised labour. What is important, however, is that the British-wide assault on organised labour by the Conservative Party was beginning to be interpreted by a significant number of Scots through a national lens. Nevertheless, most Scottish working-class hopes remained invested in that other foundational hegemonic project of the historic democratic settlement – the Labour Party. When it returned to power, the argument went, it would re-establish a fairer settlement for the entire British working class. But it would not return to power until 1997.

Notes

1 This section of the chapter draws on archival research carried out by Stephen Ashe as part of an ESRC-funded project overseen by Satnam Virdee at the Centre on Dynamics of Ethnicity (grant number: ES/K002198/1).

2 David Widgery, *The Left in Britain 1956–1968* (London: Penguin, 1976), 407.

3 This was not a new development. Previous waves of Asian, Caribbean and African migrants had also forged such cultures of solidarity. See, for example, David Featherstone, *Solidarity: Hidden Histories and Geographies of Internationalism* (London: Zed Books, 2012).

4 Indian Workers Association Archive, MS2141/A/10/3.

5 Leaflet dated 23 April 1961 – 'TUC accepts prospects of racial law' – Indian Workers Association Archive, MS2141/A/8/2/2.

6 'May Day leaflet' – Indian Workers Association Archive, MS2141/A/8/2/2.

7 Lewis V. Baldwin, Amiri YaSin Al-Hadid, Stephen W. Angell and Anthony B. Pinn, *Between Cross and Crescent: Christian and Muslim Perspectives on Malcolm and Martin* (Gainesville: University Press of Florida, 2002), 348.

8 'Black People's Alliance', *The Birmingham Post* – Indian Workers Association Archive, MS2141/A/7/4.

9 'Report of the General Secretary' (1970), 14–15 – Indian Workers Association Archive, MS2141/A/1/4; 'Black People's Alliance Aims for 1m members' – Indian Workers Association Archive, MS2141/A/7/4.

10 'Black Power at a town hall', *The Birmingham Post* – Indian Workers Association Archive, MS2141/A/7/17; see also '3,000 for city Black Youth Conference' – Indian Workers Association Archive, MS2141/A/7/17.

11 'Black Power at a town hall', *The Birmingham Post* – Indian Workers Association Archive, MS2141/A/7/17.

12 'Police save Rhodesia House from demonstrators' fury', *The Guardian*, 13 January 1969 – Indian Workers Association Archive, MS2141/A/7/19.

13 'United Black Power' – Indian Workers Association Archive, MS2141/A/7/4; 'Police save Rhodesia House from demonstrators fury', *The Guardian*, 13 January 1969 – Indian Workers Association Archive, MS2141/A/7/19.

14 Indian Workers Association Archive, MS2141/A/10/3.

15 'Sikh's plea to the race board' – Indian Workers Association Archive, MS2141/A/7/14.

16 'Now – A Demo by Immigrants', *Daily Sketch* – Indian Workers Association Archive, MS2141/A/7/14; see also 'Now – A Demo by Immigrants', *Daily Sketch*, 2 January 1969 – Indian Workers Association Archive, MS2141/A/7/2.

17 Ambalavaner Sivanandan, *A Different Hunger: Writings on Black Resistance* (London: Pluto Press, 1982), 63; Rob Waters, *Thinking Black: Britain, 1964–1985* (Berkeley: University of California Press, 2018).

18 Pratibha Parmar, 'Black Feminism: The Politics of Articulation', in *Identity: Community, Culture, Difference*, edited by Jonathan

Rutherford (London: Lawrence & Wishart, 1990); Kalbir Shukra, 'A Scramble for the British Pie', *Patterns of Prejudice* 30, no. 1 (1996): 28–29.

19 Shukra, 'A Scramble for the British Pie', 30–31.

20 Ambalavaner Sivanandan, *Communities of Resistance: Writings on Black Struggles for Socialism* (London: Verso Books, 1990).

21 Cited in Benjamin P. Bowser, Louis Kushnick and Paul Grant, 'Catching History on the Wing: A. Sivanandan as Activist, Teacher and Rebel', in *Against the Odds: Scholars Who Challenged Racism in the Twentieth Century*, edited by Benjamin P. Bowser, Louis Kushnick and Paul Grant (Amherst, MA: University of Massachusetts Press, 2004), 237.

22 There were important liberal currents of anti-racism during the 1960s and 1970s. However, the failure of the Labour Party to consistently oppose racist immigration controls and mobilise against racism explains why organisations like CARD were simply by-passed by the socialist movements discussed above.

23 Stuart Hall, Chas Critcher, Tony Jefferson, John Clarke and Brian Roberts, *Policing the Crisis: Mugging, the State and Law and Order* (London: Macmillan, 1978).

24 Nicos Poulantzas, *State, Power, Socialism* (London: NLB, 1978), 203–4.

25 Virdee, *Racism, Class and the Racialized Outsider*.

26 Hall *et al.*, *Policing the Crisis*.

27 Hall *et al.*, *Policing the Crisis*, 299.

28 Virdee, *Racism, Class and the Racialized Outsider*, 128.

29 Cited in S. Josephides, 'Principles, Strategies and Anti-Racist Campaigns', in *Black Politics in Britain*, edited by Harry Goulbourne (Aldershot: Avebury, 1990), 119.

30 Virdee, *Racism, Class and the Racialized Outsider*, 127.

31 Cited in Virdee, *Racism, Class and the Racialized Outsider*, 128.

32 Virdee, *Racism, Class and the Racialized Outsider*, 129.

33 Virdee, *Racism, Class and the Racialized Outsider*, 129.

34 Cited in Virdee, *Racism, Class and the Racialized Outsider*, 133.

35 Virdee, *Racism, Class and the Racialized Outsider*; Anitha Sundari and Ruth Pearson, *Striking Women: Struggles & Strategies of South Asian Women Workers from Grunwick to Gate Gourmet* (Chadwell Heath: Lawrence & Wishart, 2018).

36 Virdee, *Racism, Class and the Racialized Outsider*, 134.

37 For a discussion of some of the divisions that arose among Black Power, Trotskyist and other socialist currents about how

to most appropriately combat racism, see Anandi Ramamurthy, *Black Star: Britain's Asian Youth Movements* (London: Pluto Press, 2013).

38 The most important being Hall *et al.*, *Policing the Crisis*. Despite its identification of working-class and black resistance to the organic crisis of British capitalism, there is surprisingly little analysis of how these initially separate struggles became conjoined over the course of the 1970s producing remarkable criss-crossing solidarities. The political significance of this absence is that Hall *et al.* underestimate the scale of counter-hegemonic struggle.

39 Paul Gilroy, *There Ain't No Black in the Union Jack* (London: Routledge, 1987).

40 *Temporary Hoarding* magazine, 1977, cited in David Renton, *When We Touched the Sky: The Anti-Nazi League 1977–1981* (London: New Clarion Press, 2006), 33.

41 Virdee, *Racism, Class and the Racialized Outsider*, 135–38.

42 David Harvey, *The Condition of Postmodernity: An Enquiry into the Origins of Cultural Change* (Oxford: Wiley-Blackwell, 1991).

43 Andrew Gamble, *Britain in Decline: Economic Policy, Political Strategy and the British State* (London: Macmillan Education, 1994), 140.

44 Hall *et al.*, *Policing the Crisis*.

45 Bob Jessop, 'Authoritarian Neoliberalism: Periodization and Critique', *South Atlantic Quarterly* 118, no. 2 (2019): 343–61.

46 Gamble, *Britain in Decline*, 143.

47 Gamble, *Britain in Decline*, 143.

48 Stuart Hall, 'The Great Moving Right Show', *Marxism Today*, January (1979): 16–17.

49 Virdee, *Racism, Class and the Racialized Outsider*.

50 John Eldridge, Peter Cressey and John MacInnes, *Industrial Sociology and Economic Crisis* (New York: Harvester Wheatsheaf, 1991), 86.

51 Sidney Kessler and Frederic Joseph Bayliss, *Contemporary British Industrial Relations* (London: Macmillan Business, 1995), 42.

52 Eldridge *et al.*, *Industrial Sociology and Economic Crisis*, 32.

53 Simon Peplow, *Race and Riots in Thatcher's Britain* (Manchester: Manchester University Press, 2019).

54 'The "Riots"', *Race & Class* 23, no. 2–3 (1981): 223–32.

55 David Widgery, *Beating Time: Riot 'n' Race 'n' Rock 'n' Roll* (London: Chatto & Windus, 1986), 14; see also Schofield, *Enoch Powell and the Making of Postcolonial Britain* and Kundnani, 'Disembowel Enoch Powell', who both demonstrate how Thatcher studied Powell's speeches before writing her own.

56 Imogen Tyler, *Revolting Subjects* (London: Zed Books, 2013).

57 David Dixon, 'Thatcher's People: The British Nationality Act 1981', *Journal of Law and Society* 10, no. 2 (1983): 163.

58 National Centre for Social Research, *1982, British Social Attitudes Survey* (London: National Centre for Social Research, 1982).

59 Arun Kundnani, *The End of Tolerance* (London: Pluto Press, 2007).

60 One exception was the poll tax revolt throughout Britain which would so weaken Thatcher that she would be removed by her fellow Conservatives in November 1990. However, neo-liberalism with a grey face would continue under the leadership of John Major.

61 William McIlvanney, *Surviving the Shipwreck* (Edinburgh: Mainstream Publishing, 1991), 246.

4 New Labour and remaking class

The Britain that entered the 1990s had been transformed. The foundational pillars that had secured the terms of the democratic settlement were in a process of long-term disintegration. The empire was gone, and with it the economic basis for the inter-class truce described in this book. With the ascendency and then victory of neoliberalism in the 1970s and 1980s, the infrastructures of working-class power were also destroyed, and the democratic settlement thrown into a process of reversal. Was there a political force capable of arresting such developments? Where was the Labour Party in this story? Following the loss to the Conservatives at the 1992 General Election – the party's fourth successive defeat – Labour found itself confronting a profound question: would it accept the principal coordinates of neoliberal global capitalism or seek to interrupt the dismantling of the democratic settlement by rediscovering its historic mission to uplift the working class?

Such a conundrum arose against a backdrop of catastrophic defeat for the labour movement. By the early 1990s, the working class was an atomised formation that no longer held the organisational or political sway it once did. This posed a major problem not just for the labour movement but for the party that claimed to represent it. What would Labour do when its social base had fragmented revealing historic levels of class decomposition? This was the question confronting Labour at the close of the twentieth century.

As the political theorist Nicos Poulantzas observed, social democracy was thrown into a legitimation crisis by the advent of neoliberalism. It lost its class-based representational role which historically had given it legitimacy, the capacity to build consent, and ultimately, the capacity to lead in government.[1] With the working class unable to give shape and meaning to its sense of direction, the Labour Party entered into a profound and historic representational crisis: who did it seek to represent?

This also presented an opportunity, particularly for those who sought to re-invent the Labour Party and provide it with a new identity. Free of the pressures once placed on it by a thriving organised labour movement, a group of modernisers was afforded a historically unique degree of lateral movement within the upper echelons of the party to re-invent and redefine its representational role. This is precisely how New Labour emerged. At the centre of the transformation was Tony Blair, a figure who had no background in the trade unions or the public sector. In fact, Blair was markedly untouched by the 'Labourist' ethos, perhaps more so than any other leader in the party's history.[2] From the early 1990s onwards, a group of thinkers and political actors with comparatively weak ties to the organised working class began to craft a new vision of the party which became known as the Third Way.[3] What were its philosophical and political foundations?

First, and fundamentally, New Labour came into existence with the insistence that it would not seek to revive the language and politics of class. Tony Blair accepted the historic defeats of the Thatcher years and maintained there was no going back. Whatever good New Labour would do, would have to be within the new parameters set by the Conservative neoliberals that preceded him. 'I always thought my job was to build on some of the things she had done rather than reverse them,' Blair would comment later in life.[4] At the last party conference before he took office, Blair declared, 'Forget the past. No more bosses versus workers. You are on the same side. The same team.'[5] For Blair and his group of modernisers,

Labour had lost the 1992 General Election because it was too dependent on trade unions, too oriented to the working class, and too reliant on the votes from council estates. Labour had to be remade as a new party to reflect the 'realities' of Thatcherism. As one of Blair's closest aides, Philip Gould, put it in the days following the defeat of 1992, Labour had failed to relate to the fact that society was now more 'middle class', aspirational and individualistic.[6] Blair carried this analysis forward in his early interventions. In 1993, he argued that '[t]he changes in social composition, the breakup of the old class structure, mean that to form a new electoral majority the Left has to reach out beyond its traditional base.'[7]

It is important to be clear about the truths and the fiction of this analysis put forward by the modernisers. While the working class was defeated, the claim that society was now more 'aspirational' and 'middle class' was not a neutral observation, but rather a declaration of intent, an ideological construct that New Labour sought to fashion into existence through state policy. As Blair put it: 'For the new politics to succeed, it must promote a go-ahead mentality and a new entrepreneurial spirit at all levels of society.'[8] It was through this process of re-imagining that figures like Gould, Blair, Gordon Brown and Peter Mandelson ideologically re-invented the party in the 1990s.

The conception of society advanced by New Labour was characterised by a new philosophical orientation towards the concerns of the individual. It drew on work by academics such as Anthony Giddens, who declared the decline of tradition and the rise of a 'new individualism'.[9] This is traceable in the writings of key New Labour figures in the early period. For David Miliband, writing in 1994 in an important volume *Reinventing the Left*, Labour's traditional emphasis on solidarity and collectivism had to be supplemented with a new extension of what he called 'personal autonomy'.[10] Around the same time, Gordon Brown articulated a vision of an 'egalitarian socialist individualism' that rested on a 'new settlement' between the individual, market and state.

Brown envisioned an 'enabling' state that 'offered pathways out of poverty for people trapped in welfare'. The role of the government, then, would be redefined as one promoting what he called 'personal responsibility'.[11] Rather than deploy the powers of the state in the service of redistribution and equality, as it had done historically, New Labour's philosophy was organised around the idea of creating the right sorts of citizens who would be able to create the conditions of their own inclusion.[12] These themes, already evident at the very inception of New Labour, would become more pronounced after the party assumed office in 1997.

Between neoliberalism and social justice

In certain crucial respects, in its first term the New Labour government openly accepted the fundamentals of Thatcherism. This included the promotion of free market competition as the most efficient basis for capital accumulation; the privatisation of social and economic life, reducing the public sector's share of the economy; the commodification of the public sector itself; and a deep-seated commitment to globalisation.[13] This orientation to the market economy was no secret. As a Downing Street spokesperson put it succinctly in 1999: 'we are not prepared to sign up to anything that harms the City of London'.[14] Rather than renationalise industries, Blair privatised yet more still, including the nuclear fuel industry and air traffic control. Not stopping there, an extensive privatisation of public service assets was set in motion through the private finance initiative scheme, which saw schools and hospitals remodelled as semi-independent, self-financing local 'trusts', and run as if they were private companies.[15] As Eric Shaw put it, the party that once represented those sections of society disadvantaged by market forces had now come to represent those forces themselves.[16]

And yet, this was not simply Thatcher redux. New Labour's architects did believe in such a thing as 'society', and they had a conception of social justice aligned to it.[17] Blair's government introduced a set of progressive policies and measures such as tax credits, the minimum wage, support for the EU social charter, investment in schools and the health service. Further, in New Labour's first term, hereditary peerages were removed from the House of Lords, political powers were devolved to Scotland, Wales and Northern Ireland, a Greater London Assembly was formed, and initiatives such as the Human Rights Act and the Freedom of Information Act were written into the statute books. If this was neoliberalism, it was a neoliberalism of a different sort, secured, as Stuart Hall once put it, 'via the social democratic route'.[18] What was being crafted by Blair and his team was a hybrid project, one that spoke to questions of social justice on the one hand, and to a marketised individualism on the other. Neil Davidson characterised New Labour as a 'regime of consolidation', one that brought a socially democratic and therefore more ameliorative gloss to the otherwise bleak landscape of neoliberalism.[19] In this way, it was a form of social neoliberalism. With the economy booming, not just the middle class but also an asset-holding working class became significantly wealthier and felt itself to be so as consumer credit rose exponentially. This helped to forge a cross-class bloc that would sustain the party over successive general elections, despite the fact wages were not rising at the levels of the 1960s and 1970s.

The Janus-faced nature of the first New Labour government was nowhere more apparent than in the field of tackling racism. In its early incarnation, New Labour had become attractive to those interested in cultivating a politics of multiculturalism. Motivated by an ambition to move beyond the perceived failures of political blackness, these individuals saw in New Labour a vehicle for a new politics that delivered state recognition of ethnicised difference. Figures like Tariq Modood, Bhikhu Parekh and, for a while, Stuart Hall took part in debates where the politics of New Labour were formulated.[20] There were some signs that New Labour genuinely wanted to embrace the multicultural composition of modern Britain. The party leadership had committed itself to an official inquiry into the murder of Stephen Lawrence which would result in the Macpherson Report and long-awaited state recognition of institutional racism (later inscribed in law in the 2000 Race Relations Amendment Act). But running through that multicultural sensibility was a tension, as Gail Lewis notes, between 'tolerance' on the one hand and a 'desire to instil a disciplining and normalizing regime of governance' on the other.[21] Whatever commitment existed within New Labour to a politics of multiculturalism, it was never consolidated and always remained vulnerable to a retreat into racism. When Bhikhu Parekh authored a significant report on multi-ethnic Britain, that tension burst into the open. New Labour was initially supportive of the report, with Home Secretary Jack Straw declaring it 'the most important contribution to the national debate on racial discrimination for many years'.[22] The strength of Labour's commitment to multiculturalism would soon be tested, however, as elements of the report were leaked ahead of its launch. The government immediately came under pressure from a hostile right-wing press, which took umbrage at the report's anodyne observation that Britishness was still associated with whiteness. 'Now It's Racist to Use the Word "British"', decried *The Sun*.[23] More significant still was *The Daily Telegraph*, which denounced the report as an 'offence to Britain's indigenous population'.[24] Pressure began to mount on Straw, who was targeted for his initial enthusiasm for the project. At the launch of the report, Straw stepped back significantly from his earlier support, highlighting his opposition to the Commission's finding on nationalism and declaring his and the New Labour government's commitment to patriotism.[25]

This was a telling illustration, early on, of what Stuart Hall would call New Labour's 'double shuffle'.[26] The frailties of Labour's anti-racism were exposed. Later, particularly after New Labour's re-election in 2001, the party began to roll back on its uneasy and never fully fledged commitment to

multiculturalism and replace it with an assimilationist state
racism supported by imperialist wars abroad.[27]

Remaking class

One of the most radical consequences of the Blair era was
the reframing of the party's traditional representational role.
Not only did New Labour abandon the politics and language of class, it also dispensed altogether with the idea of a
working-class subject. As chief strategist Philip Gould put it,
the Labour of yesterday had failed to understand that 'the old
working class' was now 'aspiring, consuming, choosing what
was best for themselves and their families. They had outgrown the crude collectivism and left it behind in the super-
market car park.'[28] Gould, however, was wrong. The 'crude
collectivism' had not been passively outgrown but decisively
defeated by Thatcherism. What New Labour set out to do
was to erase it altogether. What did it build in its place?

Blair and his team crafted a new discourse of representational politics, one devoid of the traditional language that
had shaped the party's history since its inception. Since the
working class was no longer a cohesive social force, Labour
re-invented itself as a party of 'winners' not losers. There
was a growing emphasis on categorisations such as 'hard
working families'.[29] Distinct overtures were made to what
party modernisers called 'middle England', understood as
'aspirational' workers and swing voters in the shires and the
south-east. Over time, the party was remade, as Mandelson
put it, to become the voice of 'ordinary families who work
hard and play by the rules'.[30]

Far from an innocent response to empirical changes in
the class structure, this was a concerted attempt to remake
class itself. From the moment it assumed office, New Labour
set about achieving this mission by pitching to particular
class fractions while abandoning, indeed punishing, others.
Those who accommodated themselves to New Labour's

visions of a 'aspirational' and 'individualistically minded' working class were praised and rewarded. 'Hard working families' with assets saw their material position improve markedly. Meanwhile, those left behind were pathologised and targeted; their inability to grasp the 'opportunities' of the modern economy explained as personal failings of character and culture, not as a consequence of successive decades of neoliberalism.[31] By valorising some sections of the working class with moral worth and stigmatising others as historically out of time, Labour deepened the politics of fragmentation with profound long-term consequences. It effectively kicked away the pillar of class that had sustained the democratic settlement, removing not only a key source of its own historic legitimacy, but that of the British state as well. None of this was visible at the time, as Labour enjoyed unprecedented electoral hegemony. But its carving up of the defeated working class would in time leave the door open to competing forms of nationalism, further accelerating the historic crisis of the British state.

It was in the arena of welfare that some of the most punitive measures were enacted. In its first term, the Blair government announced a major transformation of welfare policy. Called the 'New Deal', it entailed a shift from welfare to 'workfare' – essentially, the idea that state support be made conditional on the claimant's participation in work-related activities. As Alistair Darling – then Secretary of State for Work and Pensions – put it when unveiling the welfare reform bill in 1999, there is 'no automatic right to benefit'.[32] Those who failed to take up the 'opportunities' of voluntary work, training or education risked sanctions, including loss of benefits.

This formed part of a wider project – elements of which were inherited from the Thatcher and John Major years – to remake working-class individuals as more 'employable' and less 'reliant' on state support. It entailed a break from social democratic tradition which saw welfare as a universal right for all citizens, a means of alleviating inequality through redistribution, to a new argument that put welfare in the service of a globalising economy. If individuals and their families found themselves 'excluded' from that economy (note the language and the shift away from inequality), then it was a matter of personal responsibility to find means to enter or re-enter the labour market. This represented yet another reversal of the democratic settlement, a shift from welfare to workfare: no longer a 'safety net' or a guarantee of universal rights for all, the welfare state was now refashioned as a tool in the service of the market economy. Like all forms of state intervention under New Labour, it now aimed to correct and regulate the conduct of individuals. Far from simply an economic project, this restructuring of welfare was also an attempt to fashion into existence new identities and new ways of being; or as Ray Kiely puts it, to 'make people behave in more market-conforming ways'.[33]

In particular, single parents bore the brunt of this punitive remaking of welfare, seeing their rate of income support and child benefit reduced by up to £10.50 per week if they did not 'seek work'. Defending the measures, Geoff Mulgan, Blair's Director of Policy and creator of New Labour's 'Social Exclusion Unit', argued that 'when welfare systems become more generous they tend to promote the very behaviour they are designed to alleviate ... it is wrong to make it too easy for them [single parents] to dump their children onto the responsibility of the state.'[34]

Another important policy development was the Anti-Social Behaviour Order (known popularly as the 'ASBO'). Introduced as a flagship New Labour policy on crime in July 1998, an ASBO was effectively a civil order which served to discipline 'bad behaviour' and provide morally corrective interventions for the working class (which bore the brunt of such measures). In 2002, the policy was upgraded to give landlords powers to apply for immediate court action to tackle 'yobbish' tenants.[35] The number of orders issued by Labour-controlled authorities soared during Blair's second term, rising from 427 in 2002 to an all-time high of 4,122 in

2005.[36] Blair himself described the policy as a 'personal crusade', one that ensured 'those who play by the rules do well; and those that don't, get punished'.[37] This was a punitive welfare regime that stigmatised the poorest sections of society. The state now played a formative role in mainstreaming an array of stereotypes about single mothers, 'feral' teens, 'chavs', 'broken families' and council estates as sites of idleness and delinquency – ideas which were amplified in the right-wing and tabloid press, as well as in popular culture.[38]

This was the terrain New Labour would occupy: a stigmatising politics that demonised some sections of the poor while rewarding others. By insisting that welfare reform had to reverse the 'dependency' of benefit claimants on the state, and that sections of the working class had become attached to welfare as a 'way of life', the New Labour government actively promoted some of the most pernicious tropes about working-class life. While this period undoubtedly saw parts of the so-called 'aspirational' working class enjoy greater security and economic stability, it was a political climate that produced toxic narratives of 'benefit scroungers' and targeted those who supposedly wanted 'something for nothing'. Rather than understand long-term poverty as a consequence of the ravages of globalised capitalism, New Labour instead stigmatised the most vulnerable in society and fostered a lasting set of tropes about poverty that endure today.[39]

It is no surprise, then, that the disparities established between rich and poor during the Thatcher years were consolidated under New Labour, and in fact widened. For example, the share of all capital that ended up in the hands of the top 10 per cent of income earners increased to 32 per cent, while the share of the bottom 10 per cent fell from 3 per cent to little over 1 per cent.[40] While wages rose for the large group in the middle, sections of the working class experienced a continuation of the devastating impact of the 1980s under New Labour. As divisions between classes and regions grew apace, some towns and cities fell into further decline, while others rode the wave of the economic boom.

Within just a few short years, those in the former group would become the sites of significant swings to the far right, first in the shape of the British National Party (BNP) and the United Kingdom Independence Party (UKIP), and then, most dramatically, the Brexit vote of 2016 and Boris Johnson's right-wing authoritarian march through Labour's 'red wall' in December 2019.

Transforming class into racialized ethnicity

Given that the refashioning of the democratic settlement under New Labour deepened existing divisions and engendered new stigmatisations of groups and individuals, it is no surprise that racism came to play a pivotal role in the formalisation of this new welfare regime. Counterintuitive though it may seem, Labour's early commitment to multiculturalism formed a key part of this. In refusing to revive the language of class, Labour essentially carved up the defeated working class into different ethno-racialized appellations: on the one hand there was the white working class, now racialized as white and associated with the decline and deviance of the council estate. Meanwhile, Britons of Caribbean and Asian descent were presented as classless, racialized subjects to be celebrated as multicultural British success stories or denigrated, in the case of Muslims, as 'unassimilable'.[41] Another racialized subject that emerged in New Labour discourse was the figure of the asylum seeker. In many ways, the issue of asylum provided the foil for the early New Labour government to manufacture new hostilities and appeal to long-held racisms within the electorate. As Arun Kundnani puts it:

> if the market-state was to move from welfare provision on the principles of rights and needs and instead focus on 'responsibility' and acceptance of 'shared values', then it was with asylum seekers that the gap between the old and new models seemed to be greatest. As 'aliens', they were perceived

as having no notion of responsibility to British society and no understanding of the 'values' that defined it. They were abusing the system, breaking the rules, taking advantage of 'our' generosity.[42]

Under New Labour, access to the welfare state was reconfigured along lines of national belonging, with a line of demarcation drawn between legitimate British citizens and undesirables for whom the principle of universal right did not apply. These divisions were inscribed in Labour's Immigration and Asylum Act of 1999, which saw the formation of a discrete support service for asylum seekers called the National Asylum Support Service. In this new arrangement, asylum seekers were denied access to ordinary state benefits and were instead issued with 'vouchers' which barely covered the most basic cost of survival. Prohibited from working by New Labour, asylum seekers were forced into the informal economy or resorted to begging and other perilous means of survival. This reinscribed the racist messaging of the state – that asylum seekers were scroungers who behaved in ways that were contrary to 'British' values. In a further escalation of racist state policy, New Labour then vastly expanded its programme of detention, so that asylum seekers would automatically be detained on arrival in the UK, a policy previously championed by right-wing Conservative politician Ann Widdecombe.[43] In these ways, the system reproduced asylum seekers as an unwanted excess, burden and threat. Above all, it marked asylum seekers as decidedly not 'British', and therefore not deserving of basic rights or state resources.[44]

While New Labour cultivated a specifically hostile environment for those seeking asylum, its racializing and stigmatising policies had multiple targets. In particular, the Roma community became a focus for New Labour, especially early on in Blair's first term, when hostility to Roma travellers reached fever pitch in the right-wing press. Significantly, Labour did nothing to dampen such sentiment. Just weeks after the General Election, Labour's Immigration Minister

Mike O'Brien told the *Daily Mail* in October 1997 that the Labour government would never be a 'soft touch' for 'gypsies … seeking an easy life'.[45] In 1999, Jack Straw ramped up the rhetoric further still, telling BBC radio that 'many of these so-called travellers seem to think it's perfectly ok for them to cause mayhem in an area, to go burgling, thieving, breaking into vehicles, causing all kinds of trouble, including defecating in the doorways of firms and so on, and getting away with it'.[46] In this early period, then, Labour's stated commitment to multiculturalism was bound by its much deeper attachment to nationalism. British minorities would be 'tolerated', but outsiders such as the Roma would not. As New Labour sought to remake class, it did so by identifying internal enemies against whom the model citizen was measured: on the one hand, the aspirational, consumer-minded individual seeking to advance their family's standing, versus, on the other, the feckless undesirable who ought to be excluded from access to state resources.

This class-based assault on the poor also took a more familiar racialized turn. Later in his third term, on 11 April 2007, Tony Blair gave a speech which went in search of the source of knife and gun crime in Britain. The answer, Blair suggested, was to be found in 'black culture'. 'What we are dealing with here', Blair argued, 'are specific groups or people who for one reason or another, have decided not to abide by the same code of conduct as the rest of us.' Blair was clear who he had in mind: 'we won't stop this by pretending it isn't young black kids who are doing it'.[47] After coming under criticism from anti-racist organisations, Blair doubled down, and in doing so revealed a significant building block of New Labour philosophy: 'We need to stop thinking of this as a society that has gone wrong – it has not – but of specific groups that for specific reasons have gone outside of the proper lines of respect and good conduct towards others and need by specific measures to be brought back into the fold.'[48] In many ways this captured the racist logics of the New Labour project: Blair and the modernising figures around him rejected the idea that successive decades of neoliberalism had contributed to the breakdown of social solidarity and working-class lives. Instead, the consequences of material and economic decline were explained in a racialized and stigmatising grammar. Chief strategist Philip Gould captured it well when he admitted that concern about immigration was growing under New Labour, and was increasingly seen by voters 'as a primary cause of other problems'.[49] Rather than push back against this fallacy, New Labour fully assented to it. As early as 1995, Jack Straw had asserted that 'we should not allow so much as a cigarette card to come between the Labour party and the Tory government on immigration'.[50] Once in government, both in policy and in rhetoric Blair and his cabinet pinned the blame on young black men, asylum seekers, white working-class mothers and other undesirables who refused, in New Labour language, to play by the rules.

2001: racist riots at home, imperialist wars abroad

If there was one single set of events that captured Labour's approach to 'race' and class, it was the riots of 2001. From April to July of that year, a series of urban disturbances broke out in several northern English towns (including in Oldham, Burnley and Bradford), which saw local white youths, egged on by the BNP, clashing with local Asians. These were the worst disturbances in Britain since the uprisings of 1981 and 1985. The riots of 2001 reflected the deep fragmentations and scars of neoliberalism. As Kundnani puts it, the fires in 2001 had been lit by desperation not by hope, by communities which were 'falling apart from within as well as from without … communities fragmented by colour lines, class lines … It was the violence of hopelessness. The violence of the violated.'[51] What made this possible?

The immediate clashes had been prompted by racist attacks on Asian communities and the abject failure of the police to provide any protection against this violence. But the roots were long-term and structural in origin. Amid the defeat of class and the reversal of the democratic settlement, the divide between the south-east and the rest of the country had widened, with towns and cities in the north and the midlands falling further into decline. In Burnley, wages fell and house prices plummeted during Labour's first term, leaving sections of the working class in negative equity.[52] This was at a time when nationally the trend was moving in the opposite direction. The closure of the mills left entire northern towns in long-term structural neglect. In Oldham, unemployment among young Asians reached 50 per cent by the end of Blair's first term, while in Accrington, Blackburn, Bradford and Leeds, Pakistani and Bangladeshi communities found themselves among the most impoverished 1 per cent in British society.[53] This decline inevitably came to be felt and understood through the lens of race. In parts of the working-class north, the Asian population became a signifier for the town's decline in everyday life. The figure of the 'immigrant' (always coded as black or brown) became a symbol for the very real downward mobility experienced by the working class in these areas. Though exploited by the BNP, these associations between race, space and place were crafted in the political mainstream, and by New Labour in particular.

The response of the Labour government to the riots was telling and set in motion a politics that would define the national conversation on 'race' for several years to come. Echoing the politics of several Western European states, Blair's government began to pursue an agenda that identified 'multiculturalism' as the problem.[54] Drawing on a significant report by Ted Cantle which described communities living 'parallel lives', Labour came to understand the riots as a consequence of culture rather than racism and economic decline. It was on this basis that the Home Secretary David Blunkett argued that the riots had shown the need for immigrants to understand British values and learn the English language. Blunkett spoke plainly: 'we have norms of respectability … and those who come into our home – for that is what it is – should accept those norms just as we would have to do if we went elsewhere'.[55] In the wake of this came Britishness tests and state-led demands that Asians speak English in their own homes. By suggesting that the events were caused by 'incomers' who did not understand English, the Labour government put forward the idea that the local Asian population, and specifically, the Muslim population, was somehow not 'British'.[56] What was so striking about this response was the way it elided the material decline that precipitated the disturbances and the racism that accompanied these long-term socio-economic processes. By advancing the idea that the riots were the result of 'segregation' and 'excessive diversity', the Labour government followed a familiar pattern of pathologising and stigmatising sections of the working-class poor, in particular Muslims, setting in motion a pernicious politics of Islamophobia.

The themes that surfaced in Labour's response to the riots in northern English towns in 2001 would be consolidated later that summer by a rapidly shifting geopolitical situation. The 9/11 attacks saw Blair's government acquiesce to George W. Bush's doctrine of pre-emptive strikes and regime change. On the international scene, Labour gave its full support to the 'war on terror' as an auxiliary of the United States. The launching of imperialist wars in Iraq and Afghanistan became formative moments in the consolidation of a new racialized enemy within – 'the Muslim'. From Downing Street to broadsheets, and from tabloids to television news bulletins, a political consensus emerged that increasingly legitimised claims that 'Muslim culture' and the Muslim presence more generally were in some sense incompatible with modern British values of tolerance and diversity. As a result, anti-Muslim racism formed an intrinsic justification for Labour's turn away from multiculturalism towards an assimilatory British nationalism.[57] When a 2002 white paper titled *Secure Borders, Safe Haven* repositioned New Labour as 'tough' on immigration, the drift from multiculturalism was clear to see. Now, the party made demands of minorities, and of Muslims in particular, that they assimilate into a state-conceived idea of Britishness.[58] This led some to question whether the New Labour project had a 'white heart'.[59] By the end of his tenure, in a series of lectures on 'Our Nation's Future' delivered in late 2006, Blair's intolerance had come fully into view: 'We like our diversity,' he said,

> But how do we react when that 'difference' leads to separation and alienation from the values that define what we hold in common? … [F]or the first time in a generation there is an unease, an anxiety, even at points a resentment that our very openness, our willingness to welcome difference, our pride in being home to many cultures, is being used against us; abused, indeed, in order to harm us.[60]

When the next Conservative Prime Minister, David Cameron, charged multiculturalism with perpetuating feelings of separation and racial division in 2011,[61] he was echoing a view first aired by Blair's Labour government a decade earlier.

Undoing class and the integrity of the British state

By the time Labour assumed office in 1997, the arrangements holding the democratic settlement in place were disintegrating. One pillar had been empire. The material returns of colonial extraction had improved the standard of living across Britain, binding the English and Scottish working class to the imperial project and, by extension, to Britain itself.[62] By 1997, half a century had passed since the 1947 withdrawal from India. Empire was long gone, but the unintended consequences of its demise for Britain, and in particular, the union, were only just starting to come into view. As Tom Nairn noted, when Blair's New Labour embarked on its calamitous imperial adventure in Iraq and Afghanistan, strain began to be placed on the 1707 Act of Union between England and Scotland, exposing

Britain's diminished role in the world, its failure to use the global stage to accrue prestige and confidence at home.[63]

Another pillar of the democratic settlement had been the emergence of the working class as a political force with its incorporation into the state mediated through the Labour Party. The post-war welfare settlement was the crowning achievement of this process of absorption. In particular, it played a formative role in consolidating allegiances to Britishness in Scotland.[64] What cleaved the Scottish working class to the British state was the culture and infrastructure of the labour movement.[65] Above all, it was the Labour Party that enjoyed the fruits of this symbiosis between class, state and nation. As the welfare settlement came under sustained attack from the 1980s onwards, and then later under the watch of New Labour, were allegiances to Britishness in Scotland being placed under strain?

Not immediately so. Though the foundations of the union had been shaken, Labour enjoyed near hegemony in Scotland. So far as Labourism offered a vision of a more just and equitable future for the working class, its hold on Scotland was safe. But when the two main Westminster parties began to converge both in policy and in rhetoric, the prospect of disenchantment with Labour in Scotland was heightened. The party's search for 'aspirational' white-collar and middle-class voters risked entrenching a widely held view that the Blair government was a government of the English south. Should such a perception take hold, Labour's hegemony in the English north and in Scotland could be threatened.[66] What offset this perception – at least for a decade – was devolution.

In its first term, the Blair government kept good on its promise to deliver devolution to both Scotland and to Wales. A year after assuming office, Blair ratified the result of the 1997 devolution referendum through the 1998 Scotland Act, thereby establishing a Scottish Parliament and Executive. This was the most significant readjustment in Scotland's relation to

Britain since the Act of Union in 1707. What motivated the Blair government to act in this way? Devolution in Scotland and in Wales is widely understood by the left as an act of democratisation, an exemplar of New Labour's more progressive instincts. Certainly, the convocation of a Scottish Parliament resonated as a corrective to a perceived democratic deficit after two decades of Tory rule despite only a minority of Scots ever voting Conservative. Donald Dewar, inaugural First Minister of Scotland from 1999 until his death the following year, promoted the Scottish Parliament in these ways, describing it as a 'fair and just settlement for Scotland' that would 'strengthen democratic control and make the government more accountable to the people of Scotland'.[67]

However, a quarter of a century on devolution can be more compellingly understood as a strategy of containment. There were two main elements to this process: first, devolution provided a way of ensuring the consolidation of neoliberalism in the newly formed assemblies, and second, it served as a bulwark against demands for Scottish independence. This requires some explication. As Patricia McCafferty has shown, the formation of a Scottish Parliament allowed New Labour to ostensibly address the legacy of Thatcherism in one of Labour's heartlands, but 'without dismantling the Thatcherite settlement, remaining faithful to [the] central tenets of neoliberalism'.[68] James Foley makes a similar point, suggesting that while 'grievances from the Thatcher era had inspired a sense of Scottish separateness … the institutional embodiment of these forces enshrined the essential post-Thatcherite consensus, which said nation states were powerless to shape demand or to manage the affairs of the private economy'.[69] This required careful balance on the part of the New Labour administration in Scotland: to appeal to the widely held sense that Scotland retained a social democratic disposition – in effect, an orientation to Old Labour – while simultaneously ensuring the consolidation of the New Labour project in the devolved assemblies. The Minister for Finance, Jack McConnell, exhibited this strategy in a speech to the Confederation of British Industry in 1999 where he celebrated 'the new spirit of enterprise in Scotland'. McConnell further described Scotland as 'a nation where successful enterprise and social justice can go hand in hand ... where politicians and public servants can support the wealth creation of Scottish industry and commerce'.[70] In these ways, devolution was intended to chime with New Labour's ideology of the Third Way.

This strategy of political containment would be placed under strain early on, when the first Scottish Parliament introduced free provision of personal care for older people, the abolition of tuition fees for students and the repeal of Section 28 of the Local Government Act. Tony Blair was apparently furious with this seeming breach from centralised neoliberal statecraft. 'You can't have Scotland doing something different from the rest of Britain', he complained to Liberal Democrat leader Paddy Ashdown. 'I am beginning to see the defects in all this devolution stuff.'[71] The threat to New Labour, however, was not the remnants of the party of old, but a new force in Scottish politics: the SNP. Already by 1999, the SNP was making a concerted effort to woo voters left behind by New Labour in Scotland, with party leader Alex Salmond calling for 'social democracy with a Scottish face'.[72] As Perry Anderson puts it, 'in the space created by the Blair-Brown regime, the SNP could win widespread support in attacking not only its imperial record in Iraq, but its neoliberal record at home'.[73] It was not clear in this early period of the Scottish Parliament that it would be the SNP who would enjoy the spoils of the fall of Labour. At the time, there existed an array of political projects that stood in contention: the Greens had seven Members of the Scottish Parliament returned at the 2003 election, one more than the Scottish Socialist Party.

Devolution was understood by New Labour as key to preserving the union. For Blair himself, it was intended to 'remove the danger of separatism'. George Robertson, Blair's first Minister of Defence, and later Secretary-General of NATO (and also, incidentally, Scottish himself), put it more bluntly: 'devolution', he predicted, 'will kill nationalism stone-dead'.[74] For the best part of a decade Blair and Robertson's predictions seemed to hold true. Labour retained its hegemony in Scotland's newly formed Parliament with the help of their partners in coalition, the Liberal Democrats. As a strategy of containment, devolution appeared to be working. But as Tom Nairn noted, while devolution did not immediately damage Labour's grip on Scotland, it did provide 'breathing space for new ideas to fight their way in' to the arena of Scottish public opinion, and eventually, the Parliament itself.[75] In the coming decade, those ideas would cohere around the project of Scottish independence, which threatened not only the survival of the Labour Party in Scotland, but the very integrity of the British state itself.

The defeat of class under Thatcher had set in motion a gradual but very definite process whereby the 'shared British endeavour' which had defined working-class communities in Scotland began to fade, as Allan Little puts it, 'into the middle distance of collective memory'.[76] So much of what it meant to be British in Scotland was being swept away. Eventually, that process would consume the Labour Party too.

New Labour: the slow cancellation of the future

The euphoria that accompanied the New Labour victory in 1997 reflected a genuine feeling among many that the newly elected government would reverse the ravages of 18 years of Conservative rule. Despite noticeable reforms, such as investment in schools, the introduction of the minimum wage and the devolution of political power, the excitement rapidly fell away. In theory and in practice, the New Labour government assented to the main themes of globalisation and refused to revive the project of working-class uplift, offering only a modicum of reform within the limits set by neoliberalism. What made this possible was the historic defeat of the working class under Thatcherism. It had thrown the party into a historic representational crisis: who was the Labour Party now for? For the group of modernisers who seized the moment, both the party and the working class had to be remade. Blair's government did so by fragmenting the working class even further through its welfare reconstruction project. This was a racialized politics of class that positioned certain sections of the population as problematic, ranging from white working-class council estate dwellers to Muslim others whose Britishness was always in question, and from black youths as the source of social strife to asylum seekers whose very humanity was put in doubt by the state. By locating these populations differentially through welfare policy, New Labour demarcated aspirational citizens from those who were deemed to be trapped in a 'way of life' and unable to contribute to the modernising society.[77] In so doing, it ceded ground to the right and established new hierarchies under neoliberalism.

Some Labour politicians expressed concern at this assault on working-class lives. For Peter Hain, the party's reorientation to 'Middle England' risked being 'gratuitously offensive' to its working-class base. Hain's concerns were a 'failure to deliver on housing', the 'grotesque wealth at the top' and increasing 'job insecurity'. Yet he was rebuked by one of the founders of New Labour, Peter Mandelson, who replied 'your preoccupation with the working-class vote is wrong. They've got nowhere to go.'[78] How mistaken Mandelson would prove to be. These Labour 'heartlands' would, in just a few short years, become the site of significant swings to the far right; first in the shape of the BNP and UKIP, and then, most dramatically, the Brexit vote of 2016 and Boris Johnson's hard right authoritarian march through Labour's 'red wall' in December 2019.[79] It was Blair's government that laid the ground for this. The failure to address decline and defeat, coupled with a racialized remaking of class, left the field wide open to the far right. On this terrain, Labour would soon be outflanked.

In the final analysis, Blair's achievement was to ensure that Thatcherism would exit the twentieth century not as a discredited project of the political right, but as a consolidated force in British politics for a generation to come. By the beginning of the millennium, the historic bloc of neoliberalism now included the Labour Party. At a dinner party in 2002, twelve years after she left office, Margaret Thatcher was asked what her greatest achievement was. She replied: 'Tony Blair and New Labour. We forced our opponents to change their minds.'[80]

Notes

1 Rafael Khachaturian, 'The Loss of Nicos Poulantzas: The Elusive Answer', *The Loss of Nicos Poulantzas: The Elusive Answer* (blog), 2017, www.versobooks.com/blogs/3525-the-loss-of-nicos-poulantzas-the-elusive-answer.

2 Leo Panitch and Colin Leys, *Searching for Socialism: The Project of the Labour New Left from Benn to Corbyn* (London: Verso Books, 2020), 124.

3 The New Labour modernisers were not entirely aloof from the left. Blair wrote a series of articles for the journal *Marxism Today* in 1990 and 1991, while Gordon Brown, in particular, held stronger ties to the organised working class dating back to his involvement in the miners' strike and his role in the 'Red Paper on Scotland' in 1975. See Adam McInnes, 'Deindustrialisation and Gordon Brown's approach to devolution in Scotland', *Scottish Labour History* 54 (2019): 126–53. We thank Ewan Gibbs for bringing this essay to our attention.

4 Tony Blair, 'Tony Blair: "My Job Was to Build on Some Thatcher Policies"', *BBC News*, 2013, www.bbc.co.uk/news/av/uk-politics-22073434.

5 Eric Shaw, *Losing Labour's Soul? New Labour and the Blair Government 1997–2007* (London: Routledge, 2008), 193.

6 David Butler and Dennis Kavanagh, *The British General Election of 1997* (Basingstoke: Palgrave Macmillan, 1997), 47.

7 Cited in Florence Sutcliffe-Braithwaite, *Class, Politics, and the Decline of Deference in England, 1968–2000* (Oxford: Oxford University Press, 2018), 179.

8 Tony Blair and Gerhard Schroeder, *Europe: The Third Way/Die Neue Mitte* (Johannesburg: Friedrich Ebert Foundation South Africa Office, 1998), 5.

9 Anthony Giddens, *The Third Way: The Renewal of Social Democracy* (Malden: Polity, 1998).

10 David Miliband, ed., *Reinventing the Left* (Cambridge: Polity Press, 1994), 6.

11 Gordon Brown, 'The Politics of Potential: A New Agenda for Labour', in *Reinventing the Left*, edited by David Miliband (Cambridge: Polity Press, 1994), 114. These sentiments were expressed even earlier still in 1991 by Shadow Employment Spokesperson Tony Blair in the pages of *Marxism Today*, where he argued for a 'modern view of society' and a redefining of the role of the Labour Party. For Blair, Labour ought to craft 'a new settlement between the individual and society ... so that public action is effective in achieving its objectives for the individual'. See Tony Blair, 'Forging a New Agenda', *Marxism Today*, October (1991): 32–34.

12 Alan Finlayson, *Making Sense of New Labour* (London: Lawrence & Wishart, 2003), 154.

13 Bob Jessop, 'From Thatcherism to New Labour: Neo-Liberalism, Workfarism and Labour-Market Regulation', in *The Political Economy of European Employment: European Integration and the Transnationalization of the (Un)Employment Question*, edited by Henk Overbeek (London: Routledge, 2003).

14 Cited in Shaw, *Losing Labour's Soul?*, 55.

15 Panitch and Leys, *Searching for Socialism*, 145–46.

16 Shaw, *Losing Labour's Soul?*, 5.

17 Brown, 'The Politics of Potential: A New Agenda for Labour', 118.

18 Stuart Hall, 'New Labour's Double-Shuffle', *Review of Education, Pedagogy, and Cultural Studies* 27, no. 4 (2005): 319–35.

19 Neil Davidson, 'What Was Neoliberalism?', in *NeoLiberal Scotland: Class and Society in a Stateless Nation*, edited by Neil Davidson, Patricia McCafferty and David Miller (Newcastle upon Tyne: Cambridge Scholars Publishing, 2010), 41–54; Neil Davidson, 'Neoliberal Politics in a Devolved Scotland', in *NeoLiberal Scotland: Class and Society in a Stateless Nation*, edited by Neil Davidson, Patricia McCafferty and David Miller (Newcastle upon Tyne: Cambridge Scholars Publishing, 2010), 332; Neil Davidson, 'The Neoliberal Era in Britain: Historical Developments and Current Perspectives', *International Socialism* 139 (2013), http://isj.org.uk/the-neoliberal-era-in-britain-historical-developments-and-current-perspectives/;

Neil Davidson, 'The New Middle Class and the Changing Social Base of Neoliberalism: A First Approximation', *The Oxford Left Review* (blog), 2015, https://oxfordleftreview. com/olr-issue-14/niel-davidson-the-new-middle-class-and-the-changing-social-base-of-neoliberalism-a-first-approximation/.

20 Tariq Modood, 'Ethnic Difference and Racial Equality: New Challenges for the Left', in *Reinventing the Left*, edited by David Miliband (Cambridge: Polity Press, 1994); Bhikhu Parekh, 'Minority Rights, Majority Values', in *Reinventing the Left*, edited by David Miliband (Cambridge: Polity Press, 1994); Stuart Hall and Martin Jacques, eds, *New Times: The Changing Face of Politics in the 1990s* (London: Lawrence & Wishart, 1989).

21 Gail Lewis, 'Welcome to the Margins: Diversity, Tolerance, and Policies of Exclusion', *Ethnic and Racial Studies* 28, no. 3 (2005): 543.

22 Cited in Amelia Hill, 'Racism is Institutional in Upper Tiers of British Society, Says Lord Parekh', *The Guardian*, 22 November 2010, www.theguardian.com/world/2010/nov/22/racism-instit utional-british-society-report-parekh.

23 Maya Goodfellow, *Hostile Environment: How Immigrants Became Scapegoats* (London: Verso Books, 2019), 271–72, note 1.

24 Ben Pitcher, *The Politics of Multiculturalism: Race and Racism in Contemporary Britain* (Basingstoke: Palgrave Macmillan, 2009), 40.

25 Runnymede Trust, 'Bulletin: Runnymede's Quarterly' (London: Runnymede Trust, December 2000), 4.

26 Hall, 'New Labour's Double-Shuffle'.

27 Les Back, Michael Keith, Azra Khan, Kalbir Shukra and John Solomos, 'New Labour's White Heart: Politics, Multiculturalism and the Return of Assimilation', *The Political Quarterly* 73, no. 4 (2002): 445–54, DOI: 10.1111/1467-923X.00499.

28 Philip Gould, *The Unfinished Revolution: How the Modernisers Saved the Labour Party* (London: Little, Brown & Company, 1998), 3–4.

29 Oscar Reyes, 'New Labour's Politics of the Hard-Working Family', in *Discourse Theory in European Politics: Identity, Policy and Governance*, edited by David Howarth and Jacob Torfing (London: Palgrave Macmillan UK, 2005), 231–54, DOI: 10.1057/9780230523364_10.

30 Peter Mandelson and Roger Liddle, *The Blair Revolution: Can New Labour Deliver?* (London: Faber & Faber, 1996), 17–18.

31 Mark Fisher identified this as a dominant feature of neoliberal ideology, defining it as 'magical voluntarism': 'the belief that it is within every individual's power to make themselves whatever they want to be'. See Mark Fisher, 'The Occupied Times: Good For Nothing', *The Occupied Times* (blog), 2014, https://theoc cupiedtimes.org/?p=12841. We thank Mark Rowley for bringing this to our attention.

32 Cited in Shilliam, *Race and the Undeserving Poor: From Abolition to Brexit*, 120.

33 Ray Kiely, *The Neoliberal Paradox* (Cheltenham: Edward Elgar, 2018), 156, DOI: 10.4337/9781788114424. See also Kundnani, *The End of Tolerance*, 73–74.

34 Kiely, *The Neoliberal Paradox*, 164. Mulgan also described 'those who abuse their own health when health care is socialised, safe in the knowledge that others will pick up the bill' as 'parasites' (Kiely, *The Neoliberal Paradox*, 157).

35 Alan Travis, 'Blunkett Remedy for Anti-Social Behaviour', *The Guardian*, 30 January 2002, www.theguardian.com/politics/2002/jan/30/ukcrime.immigrationpolicy.

36 'Anti-Social Behaviour Order Statistics: England and Wales 2013 Key Findings' (UK.GOV, 2014), www.gov.uk/governm ent/statistics/anti-social-behaviour-order-statistics-england-and-wales-2013/anti-social-behaviour-order-statistics-england-and-wales-2013-key-findings.

37 'Full Text: Blair on Law and Order', *BBC News*, 2004, http://news.bbc.co.uk/1/hi/uk_politics/3907651.stm.

38 The popular television programme, *Little Britain*, exemplified this trend. See Tyler, *Revolting Subjects*, 164–66.

39 See Christopher Deeming, 'Foundations of the Workfare State: Reflections on the Political Transformation of the Welfare State in Britain', *Social Policy & Administration* 49, no. 7 (2015): 862–86 for an analysis of the impact of Blair's 'work-fare' policies on public perceptions about benefits.

40 Panitch and Leys, *Searching for Socialism*, 149.

41 For a discussion on multiculturalism, race and class see Chris Haylett, 'Illegitimate Subjects? Abject Whites, Neoliberal Modernisation, and Middle-Class Multiculturalism', *Environment and Planning D: Society and Space* 19, no. 3 (2001): 351–70.

42 Kundnani, *The End of Tolerance*, 75.

43 Goodfellow, *Hostile Environment*, 99–100; Kundnani, *The End of Tolerance*, 76, 85–86.

44 Kundnani, *The End of Tolerance*, 84.

45 Goodfellow, *Hostile Environment*, 98.

46 Goodfellow, *Hostile Environment*, 99.

47 Tony Blair, 'The Callaghan Memorial Lecture' (Cardiff City Hall, 2007), http://image.guardian.co.uk/sys-files/Politics/documents/2007/04/11/blairlecture.pdf. See also Richard Seymour, *Corbyn: The Strange Rebirth of Radical Politics* (London: Verso Books, 2016), 158.

48 Patrick Wintour and Vikram Dodd, 'Blair Blames Spate of Murders on Black Culture', *The Guardian*, 12 April 2007, www.theguardian.com/politics/2007/apr/12/ukcrime.race.

49 Gould, *The Unfinished Revolution*, 493; Goodfellow, *Hostile Environment*, 275.

50 Bhikhu Parekh, *The Future of Multi-Ethnic Britain: The Parekh Report* (London: Profile Books Ltd, 2000), 226.

51 Arun Kundnani, 'From Oldham to Bradford: The Violence of the Violated', Institute of Race Relations, 2001, https://irr.org.uk/article/from-oldham-to-bradford-the-violence-of-the-violated/.

52 Mike Makin-Waite, *On Burnley Road: Class, Race and Politics in a Northern English Town* (London: Lawrence & Wishart, 2021), 134.

53 Kundnani, 'From Oldham to Bradford'.

54 Alana Lentin and Gavan Titley, *The Crises of Multi-culturalism: Racism in a Neoliberal Age* (London: Zed Books, 2011).

55 Gary Younge, 'Britain Is Again White', *The Guardian*, 18 February 2002, www.theguardian.com/world/2002/feb/18/race.politics.

56 Makin-Waite, *On Burnley Road*, 125; Pitcher, *The Politics of Multiculturalism*, 92–95.

57 Back *et al.*, 'New Labour's White Heart'.

58 Gail Lewis and Sarah Neal, 'Introduction: Contemporary Political Contexts, Changing Terrains and Revisited Discourses', *Ethnic and Racial Studies* 28, no. 3 (2005): 423–24.

59 Back *et al.*, 'New Labour's White Heart'.

60 Cited in Kundnani, *The End of Tolerance*, 91.

61 Oliver Wright and Jerome Taylor, 'Cameron: My War on Multiculturalism', *The Independent*, 5 February 2011, www.independent.co.uk/news/uk/politics/cameron-my-war-on-multiculturalism-2205074.html. On the crisis of multiculturalism in this period, see Lentin and Titley, *The Crises of Multiculturalism*.

62 On the centrality of empire to the material uplift of the working class across Britain, see Bhambra, 'Relations of Extraction, Relations of Redistribution'. See also Kojo Koram, *Uncommon Wealth: Britain and the Aftermath of Empire* (London: John Murray, 2022); Nadine El-Enany, *Bordering Britain: Law, Race and Empire* (Manchester: Manchester University Press, 2020).

63 Tom Nairn, 'Union on the Rocks?', *New Left Review* 1, no. 42 (2007): 123–24.

64 Tom Devine, *The Scottish Nation: 1700–2007* (London: Penguin, 2006), 660–61.

65 Davidson, 'Neoliberal Politics in a Devolved Scotland', 328.

66 Perry Anderson, 'Ukania Perpetua?', *New Left Review* 125 (2020): 74; Nairn, 'Union on the Rocks?', 123.

67 Patricia McCafferty, 'Working the "Third Way": New Labour, Employment Relations and Scottish Devolution' (PhD, Glasgow, University of Glasgow, 2004), 137–38.

68 McCafferty, 'Working the "Third Way": New Labour, Employment Relations and Scottish Devolution', 134.

69 James Foley, 'Europeanisation, Devolution and Popular Sovereignty: On the Politics of State Transformation in Scottish Nationalism', *Critical Sociology* 48, no. 3 (2022): 448.

70 Cited in McCafferty, 'Working the "Third Way": New Labour, Employment Relations and Scottish Devolution', 154.

71 Cited in Davidson, 'Neoliberal Politics in a Devolved Scotland', 346.

72 McCafferty, 'Working the "Third Way": New Labour, Employment Relations and Scottish Devolution', 140–41.

73 Anderson, 'Ukania Perpetua?', 86.

74 Cited in Anderson, 85, note 82.

75 Nairn, 'Union on the Rocks?', 125.

76 Allan Little, 'Scotland's Decision', BBC, 2014, www.bbc.co.uk/news/special/2014/newsspec_8699/index.html. For an excellent analysis of the defeat of class and deindustrialisation in Scotland, see Ewan Gibbs, *Coal Country: The Meaning and Memory of*

Deindustrialization in Postwar Scotland (London: University of London Press, 2021).

77 Haylett, 'Illegitimate Subjects?', 354–55.
78 Makin-Waite, *On Burnley Road*, 81.
79 Panitch and Leys, *Searching for Socialism*, 149.
80 Conor Burns, 'Margaret Thatcher's Greatest Achievement: New Labour', CentreRight, 2008, https://conservativehome.blogs. com/centreright/2008/04/making-history.html.

5   Austerity, Scottish independence, Brexit

The global financial crisis of 2007–8 was a revelatory moment that clarified how much the democratic settlement had been undermined over the past four decades. For many, the scales fell from their eyes to reveal that the prosperity of the past decade had been built on the insecure foundations of ever-increasing debt and a housing bubble. In particular, this was the moment that unmasked the degree to which Labour had committed itself to capital and the City of London. New Labour under Blair and Brown had effectively deepened the neoliberal revolution begun under Thatcher by introducing the market into health, higher education and other essential public services through private finance initiatives. If these developments had weakened the join between party and class, what allowed it to come undone was the party's response to the coalition government's austerity project. When Labour committed itself to austerity something historic occurred: working-class attachment to the institutional arrangements of the British state began to break apart. As the crisis of representation deepened further, working-class voters across Britain went in search of alternatives. The consequences of this varied dramatically across the nations: in Scotland it served as a lightning rod for independence, precipitating the dramatic rise of the SNP on a centre-left terrain; in England, meanwhile, the collapse of Labourism was to be accompanied by an authoritarian racist backlash, the exemplar of which would be Brexit. With nationalist forces of various sorts on the rise, the fragmentation of Britain began to accelerate.

The Great Recession

The recession of 2007–8 was the deepest, most sustained crisis of capitalism since the Great Depression. New Labour was still in office in what would be its third and final term. Tony Blair had been replaced by Gordon Brown, whose most decisive act as Prime Minister was to commit more than 1.162 billion pounds of public money to resuscitate collapsing financial institutions in 2008.[1] The political fall-out from rescuing Britain's banks would ultimately sink the New Labour project. At the 2010 General Election, David Cameron's Conservative Party ran for office calling for an unprecedented programme of fiscal austerity policies, at the heart of which would be a significant rollback on public spending. The crisis, they said, was Labour's making. In response, Brown meekly promised to freeze all cuts for the first 12 months, only to implement them in its second year in office if re-elected. In the party manifesto, Labour boasted of its ability to make 'tough choices': it promised 15 billion pounds in efficiency savings comprising cuts to pensions, public sector pay, welfare and local government services.[2] In essence, the choice for voters was austerity now or austerity tomorrow.

New Labour went down to a decisive defeat in 2010, losing 98 seats to rival parties – its heaviest seat loss since the party's formation. It secured just 29.7 per cent of the vote, its lowest share since 1983 and its second worst since 1918.[3] With the Labour Party a delegitimised force, David Cameron's newly assembled coalition government set about remaking the British welfare state and its public services. It did so through a brutal wave of cuts that were historic in their depth and severity. The austerity package comprised modest tax rises (just 15 per cent of the overall measures) combined with savage spending cuts

(85 per cent), the bulk of which fell on local government. As Paul Johnson, Director of the Institute for Fiscal Studies, put it in 2013, the austerity package represented 'the biggest fiscal consolidation since the war. At any other time [it] would have been considered extraordinary.'[4] The severity of the measures became clear just 90 days into the coalition government's period in office, in an emergency budget outlining cuts of 25 per cent to government departments. Local government was hit particularly hard: between 2010 and 2016, centralised funding for local government was cut by over 50 per cent and a further 30.6 per cent by 2018.[5] The human toll of these spending measures was profound: in the austerity years, half a million council workers lost their jobs,[6] 70,000 of which were in local authority adult care.[7] In total, 25 per cent of all local government positions were lost between 2009 and 2019, while in several councils the losses were as severe as 50 per cent.[8] For those who managed to retain their jobs, there was a widespread increase in precarity, with many experiencing wage freezes, pay cuts, an erosion of conditions and a rise in workloads.[9]

Meanwhile, homelessness doubled in parts of the UK, while the number of people living in poverty increased by 700,000. The unprecedented rise in the need for emergency food provision in the form of food banks was just one indication of the seriousness of the situation.[10] When the Great Recession took hold in 2008, 25,000 people in Britain were in receipt of three days' worth of emergency food; by 2014, that number had increased dramatically to more than one million.[11] Even more shocking were the 120,000 excess deaths caused by the cuts to social spending.[12] When data from the Office for National Statistics was released in 2018 showing that the growth in life expectancy in the UK was now the lowest since records began, the picture became unequivocally clear: this was an austerity that shortened lives.[13]

This joint Conservative–Liberal assault on working-class lives also had gendered consequences. When the emergency budget was announced in June 2010, a third sector feminist organisation projected that 72 per cent of the spending measures would be borne by women.[14] A combination of public sector pay freezes and rising childcare costs pushed lower-income mothers with children out of paid work. The cutbacks in public services also had disastrous effects: 31 per cent of total funds directed towards combatting domestic violence and sexual abuse funding was lost between 2010 and 2012, resulting in fewer places of refuge and support for women suffering from gender-related violence.[15] And this story was compounded by racism, as black and Asian women saw their household incomes decline significantly during the austerity years. A 2017 report by the Runnymede Trust found that Asian women in the poorest third of households lost on average 19 per cent of their income in the austerity decade from 2010 onwards, while black women lost 14 per cent on average.[16] Emejulu and Bassel outline in exemplary detail how the interlocking impact of class, gender and racist discrimination made it more likely for women of colour to be unemployed or underemployed in low-skilled low-paid work, and to be more reliant on the institutions and services of local government on account of their caring responsibilities. Overall, they concluded the austerity project was 'a slow-moving disaster for women of colour'.[17] The era of the neglectful, punitive state had arrived.[18]

New forces in the political field

After Brown's departure, new leader Ed Miliband continued his predecessor's acquiescence to the largest assault on the public sector since the Second World War. Despite the Conservative right labelling him 'Red Ed', when it came to the General Election in 2015 the main difference between the two major parties remained 'not whether to cut the welfare state but rather *how much* and *how quickly*'.[19] Even after the crushing loss in 2015, interim Labour leader Harriet Harman refused to oppose the government's cut to child tax benefits, insisting that the party had to 'be trusted on the economy'.[20]

Far from offering a robust challenge to these historic attacks on working-class livelihoods, Labour was an active participant in them. Any illusions about the Labour Party remaining a vehicle for collective working-class upliftment were extinguished in this moment. The onset of austerity represented one of those inflection points that occur in the historical lives of a social class, when it 'becomes detached from its traditional political party'. As the Marxist theorist Antonio Gramsci once observed, such crises have the capacity to open up the political field considerably, leading to delicate and dangerous situations.[21] The historically unique convergence of the three main political parties around the project of a strictly enforced austerity helped produce new forms of political polarisation. In the main, it was nationalist parties of differing sorts that seized the opportunity.

As we saw in the previous chapter, this process of political fragmentation was already in motion under New Labour. At the 1999 European elections, just two years after Labour came to power, UKIP had increased its vote from 15,000 to 696,000 and by 2004 that vote had climbed further still to 2.6 million. Alongside UKIP, the BNP saw its vote rise from 100,000 in 1999 to nearly one million in 2009. When Gordon Brown left 10 Downing Street and handed the keys to new Conservative Prime Minister David Cameron, the BNP was the fifth largest party in the UK. Though the BNP would soon collapse, the far-right surge continued. After five years of coalition government austerity and the failure of Labour to respond effectively, the UKIP vote rose dramatically in 2015 to a record 3.8 million. Across the social classes, voters were peeling away from their traditional parties, creating a space for the articulation of a resurgent nationalism. Though the BNP and UKIP secured votes in every corner of Britain, they were very much English formations responding to English questions, backed overwhelmingly by English voting publics.[22]

In Scotland, the main nationalist beneficiary of the *pensée unique* was the SNP. The erosion of the democratic settlement was keenly felt north of the border, where many believed they were increasingly disenfranchised. With the exception of the New Labour period, every Westminster election since 1979 had produced a government that lost the popular vote in Scotland. The imposition of austerity was therefore experienced by many as a project inflicted by a Conservative Party without a democratic mandate in Scotland.

One of the mechanisms that enabled Scotland to nest so comfortably within the British state was the Labour Party. Through the trials and tribulations of 18 years of Conservative rule between 1979 and 1997, the Scottish working class along with other strata continued to vote in large numbers for Scottish Labour (around 40 per cent of the popular vote, securing between 41 and 50 MPs out of 72).[23] The hope was that once returned to power, the delicate balance between the social classes encoded in the post-war welfare settlement would be restored by Labour. There remained a belief that the party's commitment to social justice would help to address some of the economic and psychic destruction experienced by large swathes of the Scottish working class. As we saw in the last chapter, this would never come to pass as Labour committed itself first to neoliberalism and then to the brutal austerity programme.

The resulting disillusionment with the Labour Party destroyed its legitimacy in Scotland. As they became increasingly detached from Labourism, working-class communities in Scotland became similarly ambivalent about the 'shared British endeavour'.[24] With industries decimated and Labour no longer committed to working-class upliftment, what was the basis of the join between party and class? So much of what it meant to be British in Scotland was being swept away. Without a natural home, the electoral allegiances of the Scottish working class were shifting. The movement for Scottish independence, once the preserve of a marginal middle class, now began to appeal to a section of disillusioned Labour voters who were growing in number.

It was in this context that the devolution settlement within the British state began to produce a set of unintended

consequences. If we recall, devolution for Blair was an instru-
ment to 'remove the danger of separatism'. A decade after
the first Scottish Parliament, it was already clear that the
reverse had occurred: devolution had effectively legitimised
the SNP and given it a political space in which to construct
an electoral alternative to Labour. Significantly, it did so
by positioning itself to the left of Labour. Though the SNP
basically accepted the major tenets of neoliberalism, it was
nevertheless able to reject some of the most hated elements of
the New Labour project by safeguarding free care for older
people, free prescriptions and a higher education without
tuition fees while also resisting water privatisation. In doing
so, it 'managed to position itself as the inheritor of the
Scottish social-democratic tradition'.[25]

The first indications of a historic shift in party affiliation in
Scotland occurred in the elections for the devolved Scottish
Parliament of 2007, where the SNP emerged as the largest
party in a minority government, dislodging Labour from
power. In 2011, it secured an overall majority with more than
44 per cent of the vote – ten points more than Scottish Labour
had ever won. With the shrunken Labour vote now dropping
to a mere 26 per cent, the SNP, led by the cultural nationalist
Alex Salmond, slowly began to pivot in the direction of Old
Labour, without ever truly occupying that ground. It did so
by carefully appealing to the disenfranchised working class
while also committing to low corporation tax to elicit the
support of business leaders, including, notoriously, Donald
Trump. In short: the SNP sought the votes without ever fully
committing to the politics of Old Labour.[26]

IndyRef

It would be in Scotland where the strength of the union
would first be tested against the new nationalist forces emergent across Britain. On 18 September 2014, the referendum
on independence was held in Scotland. Some 97 per cent of
the Scottish population had registered to vote – the highest

level of voter registration in any election since the introduction of universal suffrage in Britain. Actual turnout hit 85 per cent, a significant increase on the 65 per cent at the previous General Election in 2010. In the end, Scotland voted by 55 per cent to 45 per cent to remain within the union.[27] What this aggregate result masked was the degree to which the working class had moved towards Scottish independence. The city of Glasgow, renowned in its heyday as the 'workshop of the world', the second city of empire, chose to reject any continuing affiliation to the British state by voting 54 per cent to 46 per cent in favour of independence. The significance of class becomes clearer still when one understands that the other three regions to join Glasgow in rejecting the union were Dundee, West Dunbartonshire and North Lanarkshire – all historically seen as Labour-voting working-class strongholds.[28] The class character of the vote becomes even starker when we consider that in the bottom quartile of income, 56.4 per cent voted for independence and nearly 62 per cent of social renters voted 'Yes'. Meanwhile, just short of 65 per cent of owner-occupiers voted 'No'.[29] The movement for independence was becoming a vehicle for addressing the effects of a whole range of social and economic questions that had been blocked by the Westminster consensus: the confrontation with austerity, the relentless degradation of working-class life and imperialist wars abroad.[30] It was the Radical Independence Campaign (RIC), in particular, that gave voice to these sentiments, organising in working-class communities and helping to mobilise local campaign groups in support of independence. As the former Trotskyist turned SNP politician George Kerevan noted: 'By the end, the Yes campaign had morphed into the beginnings of a genuine populist, anti-austerity movement.'[31] The undoing of party and class was symbolically captured when Ed Miliband and Gordon Brown stood shoulder-to-shoulder with the Conservatives in backing the union, leaving many independence activists with the impression that Scottish Labour were nothing more than 'Red Tories'.[32] Changes in feelings about the nation were reflecting transformations in class experience. What allowed the case for independence to gather such traction was the way it sought to rebuild the democratic settlement rather than further dismantle it. In a curious way, then, independence set out to preserve a key element of Britishness. The post-war welfare state, the lived experience and material realities of working-class uplift were all features that had bound Scotland to the British idea over the *longue durée*. As those histories were thrown into reverse, they became the drivers of independence.

Was this mobilisation of class also a nationalist movement? Leading figures in the RIC repeatedly made the case that it was a movement largely free of nationalism. The late Neil Davidson, for example, suggested that 'for the majority of Yes campaigners, the movement was not primarily about supporting the SNP, nor even about Scottish nationalism in a wider sense'. But such a claim is untenable. The self-organised mass events on George Square in the lead-in to the 2014 referendum represented a sea of national flags. *Caledonia*, not the *Internationale*, was the main refrain. This dynamic was sustained as the large-scale mobilisations for independence were carried forward into the post-referendum years. The nationalist element, then, was evident in the mass movement for independence from its very inception in 2014. Contra Davidson, we suggest that what has happened in Scotland is that amid the historic process of de-democratisation and fragmentation, social questions have increasingly been posed in a national frame. With the decline of class as social force, an unprecedented lateral movement away from Labour and into the independence campaign occurred. Those making the journey sought to advance class interests through the project of Scottish nationalism.

If the 2014 referendum gave an indication of how many in Scotland had fallen out of love with Britain, such sentiment was reinforced at the next General Election where the SNP consolidated its hegemonic electoral rule by sending an unprecedented 56 MPs out of a possible 59 to Westminster on a 50 per cent popular vote and an anti-austerity ticket.

The surge in membership was equally astonishing. On the day of the referendum on Scottish independence in September 2014, the party boasted a membership of 25,642. By the end of that year it had soared to 94,045, and by 2018 that number would rise again to 125,482 – more than 3 per cent of the entire Scottish electorate.[33] In the meantime, Scottish Labour – long the hegemonic force in Scottish politics – went into wholesale disintegration with its popular share of the vote falling from 42 per cent in 2010 to just over 24 per cent in 2015, losing 40 seats in the process and retaining just one.

Racism and the Scottish memory hole

Given these historic events and the opening-up of political space to discuss a whole range of social questions in Scotland, it has been disappointing to find how little attention has been devoted to any serious consideration of the place of racism in this emergent splintering of the union. There are signs that this inattentiveness to racism in Scotland is being redressed in the political mainstream, to which we shall return shortly, but the conversation remains in its infancy. There has been a puzzling lack of fluency shown by the SNP and much of the Scottish left on the question of racism. Leading individuals who can make complex contributions around questions of independence, class, gender and social justice seem to fall back on simplistic sloganeering when it comes to understanding racism, and how to challenge it.

It is sobering to think, for instance, how rarely discussion about racism featured amid the political awakening that occurred during the independence campaign of 2014 and beyond, including among the Greens and socialist left. This is not new. Over many years, this relative silence has come to be interpreted as an indication of racism's absence by much of the Scottish population, including its political parties, helping to consolidate a now powerful myth that there is 'no problem here'. This is captured in that memorable phrase

'We're all Jock Tamson's bairns', an everyday saying often used to express an egalitarian Scottish outlook, translated roughly as 'we are all the same under our skin'. This narrative of an absent racism in Scottish history became even more entrenched with the rise of the SNP and Scottish independence because it was able to nest comfortably within the new common sense of Scottish politics. A dominant story has been forged by the SNP and others that the Scots are in some sense different from the English; more egalitarian and more likely to place an emphasis on collectivism over individualism, and on government intervention over self-reliance.

Regular public statements made by successive SNP First Ministers welcoming increased migration stand in stark contrast to the increasingly shrill pronouncements on migration emanating from party leaders in Westminster. On one level, such elite rhetoric is welcome. However, this mainly SNP-led re-imagining of Scotland as different (and arguably more progressive) than England/Britain has too often been crafted in such a way that the historical role played by Scotland in Atlantic slavery and colonial conquest gets consigned to what George Orwell referred to as the 'memory hole', thereby giving the impression that it never happened.[34] In the first decade of the Scottish Parliament, not a single critical comment was made by MSPs regarding Britain's historic role in slavery and empire. In more recent years, this history has been forced out into the open at Holyrood. But even then it is at times accompanied by the old claim that Scotland itself was a colony of sorts and therefore a victim as much as a perpetrator. This idea remains embedded in the SNP and in sections of the movement for independence, and indicates a hesitancy and perhaps unwillingness to truly confront the legacies of empire and racism in which Scotland is implicated.'[35] Scotland was one of the poorest countries in Western Europe in the 1690s, but by 1850 it was on the way to becoming one of the leading industrialised nations in the world. What made this possible? The trading routes established by Atlantic slavery, particularly the tobacco and sugar trades.[36]

This long-standing historical amnesia, captured by historian Stephen Mullen as 'it wisnae us',[37] has been increasingly challenged in the cultural sphere, particularly after the Black Lives Matter global protests of summer 2020. Television programmes have chronicled Scotland's role in enslavement while major institutions such as Edinburgh City Council and the University of Glasgow have undertaken initiatives to detail the way colonial plunder has shaped their activities past and present.[38] The Scottish Government has signalled its support for similar projects in the museums sector.[39] All of this is welcome. However, we should remember that the conversation remains in its infancy in Scotland. And Scottish society, unlike England, has not yet been tested on these questions. As the grim history of Scottish involvement in colonialism has been tentatively brought into view, some have responded with predictable defensiveness. Attempts by Edinburgh City Council to draw attention to the role of Henry Dundas in delaying the abolition of enslavement have been resisted by some of Scotland's most senior academics. Similarly, efforts by the University of Edinburgh to confront legacies of colonialism within the institution have been challenged by members of its staff.[40] If inertia and denial characterise one set of responses, outright racist backlash can be found in society at large. When the Edinburgh-based Mercury Prize winning band Young Fathers had the temerity in 2017 to make a video in the National Portrait Gallery commentating on whiteness and representation, a wave of racist hate followed. 'Go back to your mudhut-culture', posted one respondent on Facebook. Another wrote 'Why do you have a black man chimping out in a museum?'[41] Should anyone need reminding, social attitudes on racism remain broadly similar in Scotland to other parts of Britain.[42]

It is crucial to remain alive to the disjuncture between elite discourse on migration and the lived reality of racialized minorities in Scotland. Everyday racism remains a deeply structuring force distorting the lives of those we know as the black and brown Scots. From racist harassment in the community, to systematic discrimination in the workplace, so-called new Scots remain a class apart; one that is seen as somehow not quite Scottish.[43] And on occasions, just as in England, this failure to imagine this group of Scots as 'truly Scottish', as 'unhyphenated Scots', can lead to violence and sometimes murder. From the racist killing of Surjit Singh Chhokar just prior to the advent of devolution in 1998 to the death of 31-year-old Sheku Bayoh while being restrained by 15 police officers in Kirkcaldy, Fife in May 2015, violent racism remains a significant ongoing problem in Scottish society, irrespective of the other more progressive transformations that have been in motion. So, when sympathetic public statements made by elite politicians in Scotland about migration and the 'new Scots' are taken at face value – including by parts of the left – this carries with it the danger of underestimating and thereby disarming the contemporary struggle against racism that is required.

In recent years in Scotland, concerns about growing class inequalities have come to be expressed through the national question but they have not been accompanied by any significant shift in consciousness on challenging racism, including anti-Irish racism, which was long a dominant form of discrimination in Scottish society.[44] We need to come to terms with the historical and contemporaneous legacy of racism in Scotland and find ways of challenging its corrosive effects. In a nation such as Scotland, we cannot foreground questions of democratisation and social justice by going around race; we have to go through race.

An important step might be to recognise not only the ethnic diversity of Scotland's working class, but also to actively build more concrete alliances and coalitions with those civil society organisations created by black and brown Scots and migrant communities in the course of their attempts to challenge racism and secure a more stable life for their children and grandchildren. This has the potential to expand the political imaginary of all social movements. And it can draw on recent successes. When a Home Office van appeared on Kenmure

Street in the southside of Glasgow in May 2021, word quickly spread that two Indian men were facing deportation. Local campaigners gathered and within a few hours, hundreds of Glaswegians took over the street, demanding that the immigration raid be stood down. 'These are our neighbours, let them go!' was the chant. Activist-scholar Smina Akhtar describes the scene: 'young girls dressed up in their new Eid clothes were in the street with home-made banners, a local bakery donated an Eid cake for the protesters, local shops brought down snacks and water whilst a local gym allowed protesters to use their toilets'.[45] Remarkably, the protesters won, and the two men were released back into their community to rapturous applause. The event showed the potential of everyday anti-racism from below. As Britain fragments, Scotland has a rare opportunity to un-think the old way of doing emancipatory politics; will the future belong to Kenmure Street or the more familiar tale of denial and indifference?

Brexit

Following quickly on the heels of the 2014 Scottish independence referendum was the 2016 referendum on Britain's secession from the transnational union of the EU. There was already strong evidence from the 2015 General Election about the continuing rightward drift in English politics accompanied by the loosening of attachments between party and class. Around half of skilled, semi-skilled and unskilled workers voted either Conservative or UKIP at the election compared with just 30 per cent for Labour.[46] That is, around half of the working class were aligned to the politics of the Conservative Party and the far right, indicating the political consequences of a long-term realignment of class.

This fragmentation rebounded in reaction and racism during the Brexit referendum. On 23 June 2016, the British voted narrowly to secede from the EU by 52 per cent to 48 per cent. Although a British event, there is a compelling case to centre the English story in Brexit. The vote to leave in England was higher than in other nations (53.6 per cent). The 'Englishness' of Brexit was also traceable in the way many Leave voters defined their national identity. Seventy-nine per cent of those who identified as 'English not British' voted Leave as did 66 per cent of those who identified as 'more English than British'.[47] What gave shape to this idea of the nation? In the lead-in to Brexit, large-scale survey data indicated that the main drivers of political Englishness were Euroscepticism and concern about 'immigration'.[48] Among the myriad of factors propelling Britain towards secession from the EU in 2016 was the invisible driver of Englishness. But what else made possible this historic vote?

The relatively unexpected victory for the Leave campaign led many to go in search of possible explanations. What quickly emerged were competing claims about the role of class. For some, the result was decided by those same social forces that had voted for UKIP at the 2014 European Parliament elections, that is, 'the vote for Brexit was delivered by the "left behind" … pensioners, low skilled and less well-educated blue-collar workers and citizens who have been pushed to the margins'.[49] Meanwhile, some postcolonial sociologists questioned the place of the working-class vote in the events of June 2016, suggesting instead that it was the 'middle class' that delivered Brexit, not the white working class as claimed by many commentators.[50] This claim is predicated on an analysis informed by the widely used National Readership Survey (NRS) definition of class, which designates the working population into the following six categories: A, B and C1, C2, D and E.[51] Understood from this perspective, while two-thirds of those who voted in the lowest two social classes (D and E) chose to leave the EU,[52] these two groups represented just 24 per cent of the overall proportion of Leave voters.[53] It was the ostensibly middle-class categories that were crucial to the final outcome, the data suggests, with almost three in five Leave votes coming from those in social classes A, B and C1.[54] However, such analyses rest on a definition of the working class as the old unskilled and semi-skilled manual workers (understood here as D and E). What this ignores is what we might term the white-collar proletariat that is found in the purportedly middle-class category of C1, as well as the skilled manual working class to be found in category C2. Between 40 per cent and 66 per cent in these social classes voted for Brexit. Contrary to the accounts above, then, we want to insist that the working-class vote was indeed central to Brexit. Additionally, age was also a key feature of the Brexit vote. While 62 per cent of 25–34-year-olds chose to Remain, 60 per cent of those aged 65 and over voted to Leave. In sum, it is too simplistic to suggest, on the one hand, that Brexit constituted the revolt of the 'left behind' or, on the other, that it was delivered by the 'middle class'. Rather, what needs to be understood is how the campaign to Leave managed to successfully cohere a significant cross-class coalition of middle-aged and older men and women, among whom, the working-class vote was crucial.[55]

If Brexit was a story about class, it was also a story about racism. This was confirmed in the wave of racist hate unleashed against migrants as well as the long-established black and brown British that followed in the wake of the vote. More than 6,000 racist hate crimes were reported to the National Police Chiefs Council in the four weeks after the referendum result was declared.[56] Incidents ranged from physical assault and property damage to verbal abuse. One individual recalled being referred to as 'dirty Paki scum' and taunted about how 'Pakis need to be rounded up and shot'. A Sikh radiographer recounted how a patient asked 'Shouldn't you be on a plane back to Pakistan? We voted you out.' In 51 per cent of the incidents, perpetrators referred specifically to the referendum in their abuse, with the most commonly involved phrases including 'Go Home' (74 stories), 'Leave' (80 stories) and 'fuck off' (45 stories). These were followed up by statements such as 'We voted you out', 'We're out of the EU, now we can get rid of your lot', 'When are you going home?' and 'Shouldn't you be packing your bags?' And then, in August 2016, six teenage boys were arrested in Harlow, Essex, for a brutal street attack on an Eastern European migrant after he was heard speaking Polish in the street. The man subsequently died. What is striking about this wave of racist violence was the way its perpetrators made little attempt to distinguish between black and brown citizens and white European migrants – in their eyes, they were all racialized outsiders.[57]

How can it be that the first formal break from the 30-year neoliberal consensus was marbled through with such racism and violence, especially in England? How was such a political terrain crafted that saw a majority of the English population vote for Brexit visions that were stained through with a desire to recover former glories of empire, on the one hand, and the promise to pull up the proverbial drawbridge in order to drastically reduce migration on the other? The answer to these questions can be found in British decline and the defeat of the working class.

Defeat and decline in England

Political reaction in England in the current moment asserts itself against a backdrop of the erosion of the democratic settlement. Britain has undergone a painful process of structural decline since the late 1970s and the onset of neoliberalism. Since the defeat of the multiple socialist projects of hope, the prospect (and brutal realities) of downward mobility have produced class injuries and collective experiences that have been recast through the politics of *ressentiment*.[58] In this context, decline, though necessarily a multi-ethnic process, is experienced in a racialized frame and is increasingly responded to by some sections of the working class through the politics of resentful English nationalism.[59] The realignment of politics to the right has therefore created an environment in which racism can be more readily articulated since it resonates with the cultural and political logic of our time. It speaks to people 'where they are at'.

This racializing nationalism has borne a particularly defensive character in England since the 2008 crisis, as we have mapped in this book. It is defined not by imperial prowess or superiority, but by a deep sense of loss of prestige; a retreat from the damaging impact of a globalised world that is no longer recognisable, no longer 'British'. The decline of empire, then, has not led to the overcoming of the English imperial complex, but its retraction into a defensive exclusionary imaginary: we are under siege, it is time to pull up the drawbridge. This Powellite vision of Brexit held at its centre a story about immigration in which the migrant was presented not just as an economic threat, but also as a security threat. This argument was made most powerfully in the lead-in to the Brexit vote, when Nigel Farage stood before a Leave EU campaign poster which pictured Middle Eastern refugees queuing at Europe's borders under the slogan 'Breaking Point'. The subheading read: 'We must break free of the EU and take back control.' The message was clear: if Britons voted leave, we could successfully keep such people from entering the country. Stuart Hall once remarked that 'Englishness has always carried a racial signature'.[60] We heard its familiar refrains in the crisis of Brexit.

Decline and defeat have been accompanied by a powerful narrative, produced by New Labour and Conservatives alike, which understands the principal losers from globalisation to be the 'white working class'.[61] And this message has been amplified over and again by the right-wing press who deploy this category for their own instrumental ends, particularly for eroding support for multiculturalism.[62] As a result, the white working class – a descriptive and analytic category whose origins lay in social science research – has been brought to life as a collective social force in the Thompsonian sense, such that some working-class men and women now understand and make sense of the real economic pain they suffer through such a racialized frame of victimhood.[63]

This construction of the category of white working class has led to a number of deleterious developments in the field of politics. First, it has helped cohere and shift sections of the working class into the camp of the anti-immigrant right;

that is, they have come to invest politically in understanding themselves as a white working class and as the main victims of globalisation. Second, by juxtaposing the category white working class to immigrant, such a narrative not only privileged one stratum of Britain's working class over the other on the grounds of citizenship, it also erased those parts of the working class who are black and brown Britons. And through this sleight of hand, the lived experiences of those whose economic austerity was overlain by race and gender discrimination were simply elided[64] and closed off from public scrutiny and debate. Third, and related, this had the effect of further dividing the multi-ethnic working class on racialized lines, and in doing so submerged those other explanations for the decline in living standards – for example, the austerity imposed by Labour and Conservative elites alike.

The consequences of these developments for socialist politics in England have been catastrophic. Today, working-class pain – which, necessarily, is a multi-ethnic pain – has come to be understood by substantial numbers of mainly older people through a racialized anti-immigrant lens. The long-term absence of multi-ethnic class narratives and erosion of working-class agency, combined with New Labour attempts to racialize class politics and its subsequent complicity in imposing austerity, helped carve open this space for the injuries of class to be recast through the politics of racist resentment. And it has driven the process of fragmentation, producing the event we now know as Brexit.

Once the Brexit vote is analysed town by town, what is striking is just how closely it maps onto those working-class communities that went down to a series of historic defeats in the 1980s at the hands of the neoliberal counter-revolution. Typical are the former mining towns from Barnsley to Bolsover, Rotherham to Doncaster, who felt the full force of Thatcherism during the 1984–5 miners' strike and the subsequent destruction of industry. Former steel towns like Redcar and Scunthorpe, along with others like Hull and Grimsby, once home to thriving fishing industries, all voted strongly to leave, as did a string of former mill towns in Lancashire. And should anyone think this represented a north–south divide, one could point to the 'garden of England', Kent, where towns like Gravesend, Gillingham, Chatham and Dartford – once home to powerful groups of workers employed in cement manufacture, paper mills, coal mines, the railways and the Royal Navy dockyard – all voted over-whelmingly for Brexit.[65]

Brexit also defined the 2019 General Election, not just the tone and content of the campaign, but also its outcomes.[66] The Conservatives held all of their Leave-voting seats and gained 55 more, boosting their share of the Leave vote to 74 per cent in the process. In contrast, the only seat that Labour managed to gain in 2019 is one that had voted Remain while 52 of the 60 seats it lost were Leave-voting.[67] Central though it was, the role of Brexit was less cause than it was effect; the election represented longer-term trends that we have identified here. In 2010, Labour was still outperforming the Conservatives in its working-class heartlands. The austerity years saw those margins wither away as Labour suffered a historic crisis of legitimacy and representation. A leftward turn in 2017 under the leadership of Jeremy Corbyn proved to be the exception rather than the rule; after a decade of Conservative governance and unprecedented austerity measures, working-class support for Labour continued its secular decline, culminating in the devastation of the 2019 election where even the blue-collar vote in the historic heartlands was lost.[68] A combination of abstention (which was higher in working-class areas), class decomposition and realignment spelled disaster for the party and the Corbyn project.

Despite these historic transformations, some on the left saw in Brexit a potential opening for socialists. There are two key elements to this argument. First, they point out, rightly, that the EU is not the formation its progressive champions imagine it to be. While 'freedom of movement' is granted to some, it is denied to many more. The EU has been crafted into a

Fortress Europe that effectively acts as a militarised and racist bordering regime. The mass graves of drowned migrants at the bottom of the Mediterranean Sea are testament to the devastating consequence of EU policy in this area. As Malik puts it: 'Fortress Europe has created not only a physical barrier around the continent, but an emotional one, too, around Europe's sense of humanity. Migrants [from outside the EU] have come to be seen less as living, breathing human beings than as so much flotsam and jetsam to be swept away from Europe's beaches.'[69] Second, those on the left who supported Brexit did so because they understood it as a defeat for the transnational ruling elites and the neoliberal settlement. They viewed it as a blow delivered by a working class finally waking up to the profoundly undemocratic nature of EU structures and the suffering they have caused.

While we share their criticisms of 'Fortress Europe', we cannot agree Brexit represents a progressive development. Instead, we see the outcome of the 2016 EU referendum as but one swell in a tide of reactionary populism that has swept the European mainland and other parts of the globe over the past decade.[70] It demands nothing less than a restoration of a mythic golden age of sovereign nation-states defined by cultural and racial homogeneity. In England, it has been the far right, first and foremost, that has capitalised on the breakdown of the neoliberal consensus amid a severe financial crisis and the resultant imposition of austerity.[71] And in the fragmentation that has ensued, a sizeable fraction of the working class has been cohered around these ideas. There is little to celebrate in this.

Britain fragmented

British national consciousness was sustained over much of the twentieth century by the dual pillars of the Conservative and Labour parties combined with the economic returns of empire. The post-war welfare settlement was the crowning achievement of this century-long process. But as these pillars have crumbled, a dramatic realignment has occurred, producing a crisis of legitimacy in the institutions of the British state. This historic unravelling has left a fragmenting Britain that is breaking at the seams. What had once given it stability has been swept away. Secessionism, nationalism and fragmentation are what remains.

The austerity decade crushed any lingering hopes that these processes could be halted. As the New Labour era drew to a close, many were left with the feeling that there was no alternative to the political status quo. This was an era characterised by 'depoliticisation', even 'anti-politics'.[72] The failure of Labour to offer any respite to the punishing years of austerity under the coalition government served only to consolidate those feelings. As the crisis unfolded after 2008, multiple cracks appeared in the system as the join between party and class came undone. This drove the emergence of nationalist projects of varying sorts, but in particular, Brexit and Scottish independence. The tectonic shifts in voter allegiances that had been underway but had not yet become visible now burst into view. The Scottish independence referendum opened up a possibility of a break from political stalemate at Westminster, inspiring movements for social justice in Scotland and beyond, including the early Corbyn surge in England. But the campaign for Scottish independence was not without its discontents. In particular, its silence and inertia on the question of racism were characteristic of a long-held Scottish disposition that continues to this day. Brexit, meanwhile, channelled rage of a different sort, providing an outlet for a right-wing populist backlash against an out-of-touch political elite, a backlash that frequently manifested in racist reaction.

Both Brexit and the movement for Scottish independence signalled how social and economic injustice would be responded to in constitutional terms, through national questions and the politics of secessionism. Similarly, they revealed how intergenerational inequalities increasingly define the landscape in Britain. In the Scottish independence referendum, the vote against secession was heavily weighted towards older people, with a clear majority of over-55s voting 'No', including nearly three-quarters of over-65s. Those under 40 voted in their droves for Yes, with 59 per cent of 25–34-year-olds voting for independence.[73] The fragmentation unfolded generationally in Brexit, too, as under-40s leading increasingly precarious lives voted in their millions for Remain, while older, asset-holding members of the working class opted to Leave. In some respects, the Corbyn project maps onto this pattern: Labour secured the vote of the youth in 2017 and 2019, but was sunk by its losses among older working-class voters. As younger voters stared into the future and saw nothing but instability and precarity, they voted for projects of hope (Corbynism and Scottish independence). Meanwhile, older working-class voters either abstained in the post-austerity years or leaned towards authoritarian right-wing projects such as Brexit or the Conservatives. What will be the long-term political home for these populations? Who will give political expression to these intergenerational divides and the material inequalities that produce them? The answers to these questions will determine the future of a fragmenting Britain that lurches from one crisis to the next.

Notes

1 'Taxpayer Support for UK Banks: FAQs – National Audit Office (NAO)', National Audit Office, 2020, www.nao.org.uk/high lights/taxpayer-support-for-uk-banks-faqs/.

2 *The Labour Party Manifesto 2010: A Future Fair for All* (London: The Labour Party, 2010), 6.

3 Philip Cowley and Dennis Kavanagh, *The British General Election of 2010* (Basingstoke: Palgrave Macmillan, 2010), 340.

4 Paul Johnson, 'Spending Review 2013: Opening Remarks', 27 June 2013, https://ifs.org.uk/publications/6775.

5 Sarah-Marie Hall, Kimberly McIntosh, Eva Neitzert, Laura Pottinger, K. Sandhu, Mary-Ann Stephenson, Howard Reed and Leonie Taylor, 'Intersecting Inequalities: The Impact of Austerity

on Black and Minority Ethnic Women in the UK' (London: Runnymede Trust, Women's Budget Group with RECLAIM and Coventry Women's Voices, 2017), 4, www.semanticscholar. org/paper/Intersecting-Inequalities%3A-The-Impact-of-Auster ity-Hall-McIntosh/993edd118bc751e13c137462563eb2c58 c1c9ffa.

6 'Cuts to Local Services', UNISON The Public Service Union, 2014, www.unison.org.uk/at-work/local-government/key-issues/ cuts-to-local-services/.

7 Richard Vize, 'Public Sector Workers Have Been Pummelled by Austerity. It's a Scandal', *The Guardian*, 1 October 2018, www.theguardian.com/society/2018/oct/01/public-sector-work ers-pummelled-austerity-scandal.

8 Eichler William, 'Around 25% of Local Government Jobs "Slashed" Due to Austerity', *LocalGov.Co.Uk* (blog), 2019, www.localgov.co.uk/Around-25-of-local-government-jobs-slas hed-due-to-austerity/47647.

9 Annette Hastings and Maria Gannon, 'Frontline Public Sector Workers Acted as "Shock Absorbers" of the Austerity Cuts to Local Government Budgets', *LSE British Politics and Policy* (blog), 2021, https://blogs.lse.ac.uk/politicsandpolicy/frontline- public-sector-workers-austerity/.

10 'The True Cost of Austerity and Inequality – UK Case Study' (Oxfam International, 2013), www-cdn.oxfam.org/s3fs-public/ file_attachments/cs-true-cost-austerity-inequality-uk-120913- en_0.pdf.

11 Gloria Tyler, 'Food Banks in the UK' (London: House of Commons Library, 2021), https://commonslibrary.parliament. uk/research-briefings/cbp-8585/.

12 Johnathan Watkins, Wahyu Wulaningsih, Charlie Da Zhou, Dominic C. Marshall, Guia D. C. Sylianteng, Phyllis G. Dela Rosa, Viveka A. Miguel, Rosalind Raine, Lawrence P. King and Mahiben Maruthappu, 'Effects of Health and Social Care Spending Constraints on Mortality in England: A Time Trend Analysis', *BMJ Open* 7, no. 11 (2017): e017722, DOI: 10.1136/ bmjopen-2017-017722.

13 Amelia Hill, 'UK Life Expectancy Improvement Has Stalled, Figures Show', *The Guardian*, 25 September 2018, www.theg uardian.com/science/2018/sep/25/improvement-uk-life-expecta ncy-stalled-ons-figures-show. See also Gerry McCartney, David Walsh, Lynda Fenton and Rebecca Devine, *Resetting the Course*

for Population Health: Evidence and Recommendations to Address Stalled Mortality Improvements in Scotland and the Rest of the UK, May 2022, Glasgow Centre for Population Health, Glasgow, www.gla.ac.uk/media/Media_852696_smxx.pdf.

14 See report by Fawcett Society in Hazel Conley, 'Using Equality to Challenge Austerity: New Actors, Old Problems', *Work, Employment and Society* 26, no. 2 (1 April 2012): 349, DOI: 10.1177/0950017011432906.

15 Hazel Conley, 'Economic Crisis, Austerity and Gender Equality: The UK Case', *European Gender Equality Law Review* 2 (2012): 17.

16 Hall *et al.*, 'Intersecting Inequalities', 3.

17 Akwugo Emejulu and Leah Bassel, 'Austerity and the Politics of Becoming', *Journal of Common Market Studies* 56, no. S1 (2018): 110–11, DOI: 10.1111/jcms.12774; Akwugo Emejulu and Leah Bassel, 'Minority Women, Austerity and Activism', *Race & Class* 57, no. 2 (1 October 2015): 86–95, DOI: 10.1177/0306396815595913. For more on the impact of austerity on women of colour, see Hall *et al.*, 'Intersecting Inequalities'. On the racist consequences of the austerity decade more generally, see Nasar Meer, *The Cruel Optimism of Racial Justice* (Bristol: Policy Press, 2022), 61–62.

18 Gargi Bhattacharyya, Adam Elliott-Cooper, Sita Balani, Kerem Nisancioglu, Kojo Koram and Dalia Gebrial, *Empire's Endgame: Racism and the British State* (London: Pluto Press, 2021), 7–8.

19 Emejulu and Bassel, 'Minority Women, Austerity and Activism'. Emphasis original.

20 Patrick Wintour, 'Anger after Harriet Harman Says Labour Will Not Vote against Welfare Bill', *The Guardian*, 12 July 2015, www.theguardian.com/politics/2015/jul/12/harman-labour-not-vote-against-welfare-bill-limit-child-tax-credits.

21 Antonio Gramsci, *Selections from the Prison Notebooks*, edited by Quintin Hoare and Geoffrey Nowell-Smith (London: Lawrence & Wishart, 1971).

22 Although ostensibly a Unionist party, the UKIP project was predicated on a distinct politicisation of Englishness. This is reflected not only in the composition of the UKIP vote (more than 90 per cent of the party's 3.8 million votes in 2015 were cast in England), but in attitudinal studies of those voters, who strongly identified as English rather than British. See Richard

Wyn Jones, Guy Lodge, Ailsa Henderson and Daniel Wincott, 'The Dog That Finally Barked: England as an Emerging Political Community' (London: Institute for Public Policy Research, 2012), 33, www.ippr.org/research/publications/the-dog-that-finally-barked-england-as-an-emerging-political-community; Richard Hayton, 'The UK Independence Party and the Politics of Englishness', *Political Studies Review* 14, no. 3 (2016): 406. On the mainstreaming of the BNP and UKIP, see Aurelien Mondon and Aaron Winter, *Reactionary Democracy: How Racism and the Populist Far Right Became Mainstream* (London: Verso Books, 2020), 40–49.

23 David Butler and Dennis Kavanagh, *The British General Election of 1979* (Basingstoke: Palgrave Macmillan, 1980); David Butler and Dennis Kavanagh, *The British General Election of 1983* (Basingstoke: Palgrave Macmillan, 1985); David Butler and Dennis Kavanagh, *The British General Election of 1987* (Basingstoke: Palgrave Macmillan, 1988); David Butler and Dennis Kavanagh, *The British General Election of 1992* (Basingstoke: Palgrave Macmillan, 1993).

24 Little, 'Scotland's Decision'. As Gibbs has shown, deindustrialisation served as a catalyst for dislocating Scottish and British identity, and for the growth in demands for increased Scottish political autonomy from Westminster. See Gibbs, *Coal Country: The Meaning and Memory of Deindustrialization in Postwar Scotland*.

25 Neil Davidson, 'A Scottish Watershed', *New Left Review* 1, no. 89 (2014): 12. For a searing critique of the record of the SNP in government see Cailean Gallagher, Amy Westwell and Rory Scothorne, *Roch Winds: A Treacherous Guide to the State of Scotland* (Edinburgh: Luath Press Ltd, 2016).

26 Ben Jackson, *The Case for Scottish Independence: A History of Nationalism Political Thought in Scotland* (Cambridge: Cambridge University Press, 2020).

27 Davidson, 'A Scottish Watershed', 21.

28 David Featherstone, 'Revolt on Clydeside? Space, Politics and Populism', *Geoforum* 62 (2015): 194.

29 Foley, 'Europeanisation, Devolution and Popular Sovereignty', 450.

30 On working-class experiences of widening inequalities in Glasgow, the epicentre of the independence surge in 2014, see Kirsteen Paton, *Gentrification: A Working-Class Perspective* (London: Routledge, 2014).

31 Davidson, 'A Scottish Watershed', 15. Others have traced these developments back further still, suggesting contemporary Scottish nationalism has long been associated with a moral critique of neoliberalism and a defence of the welfare state. See Jonathan S. Hearn, *Claiming Scotland: National Identity and Liberal Culture* (Edinburgh: Polygon at Edinburgh University Press, 2000).

32 David Featherstone, 'From Out of Apathy to the Post-Political: The Spatial Politics of Austerity, the Geographies of Politicisation and the Trajectories of the Scottish Left(s)', *Environment and Planning C: Politics and Space* 39, no. 3 (2021): 480.

33 Lukas Audickas, Noel Dempsey and Philip Loft, 'Membership of UK Political Parties', House of Commons Library, 2019, https://commonslibrary.parliament.uk/research-briefings/sn05125/.

34 For a detailed analysis of the emergence of the idea of a 'civic' Scotland purportedly more open and egalitarian than England, see Jackson, *The Case for Scottish Independence*.

35 See Mullen, Stephen and Gibbs, Ewan, 'Scotland, Atlantic Slavery and the Scottish National Party: From colonised to coloniser in the political imagination' *Nations and Nationalism* (2023), 9, 11.

36 Stephen Mullen, 'Ae Fond Kiss, and Then We Sever!', *Variant* 35 (2009): 8. On Scotland and empire see Bryan Glass, *The Scottish Nation at Empire's End* (Basingstoke: Palgrave Macmillan, 2014); Bryan Glass and John M. MacKenzie, eds, *Scotland, Empire and Decolonisation in the Twentieth Century* (Manchester: Manchester University Press, 2015); John M. MacKenzie and Tom Devine, eds, *Scotland and the British Empire* (Oxford: Oxford University Press, 2016); Stephen Mullen, 'Centring Transatlantic Slavery in Scottish Historiography', *History Compass* 20, no. 1 (2022).

37 Stephen Mullen, *It Wisnae Us: The Truth About Glasgow and Slavery* (Edinburgh: The Royal Incorporation of Architects in Scotland, 2009).

38 See 'Edinburgh Slavery and Colonialism Legacy Review', The City of Edinburgh Council, 2021, UK, www.edinburgh.gov.uk/edinburghslaverycolonialism; 'Historical Slavery Initiative', University of Glasgow, 2021, www.gla.ac.uk/explore/historicalslaveryinitiative/. See also David Alston, *Slaves and Highlanders: Silenced Histories of Scotland and the Caribbean* (Edinburgh: Edinburgh University Press, 2021); Kate Phillips, *Bought & Sold: Scotland, Jamaica and Slavery*

(Edinburgh: Luath Press, 2022); and Stephen Mullen, *The Glasgow Sugar Aristocracy: Scotland and Caribbean Slavery, 1775–1838* (London: University of London Press, 2022).

39 'Empire, Slavery & Scotland's Museums', Museum Galleries Scotland, 2021, www.museumsgalleriesscotland.org.uk/proje cts/empire-slavery-scotlands-museums/.

40 On Dundas, see Stephen Mullen, 'Henry Dundas: A "Great Delayer" of the Abolition of the Transatlantic Slave Trade', *The Scottish Historical Review* 100, no. 2 (2021): 218–48.

41 'Young Fathers Suffer Backlash over Art Galleries Criticism', 2017, www.scotsman.com/arts-and-culture/young-fathers-suffer-backlash-over-art-galleries-criticism-1443792.

42 '30 Years of British Social Attitudes Self-Reported Racial Prejudice Data' (London: NatCen Social Research, 2014), www. bsa.natcen.ac.uk/media/38110/selfreported-racial-prejud ice-datafinal.pdf; 'Scottish Social Attitudes 2015: Attitudes to Discrimination and Positive Action' (Scottish Government, 2016), www.gov.scot/publications/scottish-social-attitudes-2015-attitudes-discrimination-positive-action/.

43 On everyday racism in Scotland, see Crown Office and Procurator Fiscal Service, 'Hate Crime in Scotland 2020–21' (Edinburgh, 2021), www.copfs.gov.uk/about-copfs/news/hate-crime-in-scotland-2020-21/. On race equality and elite political actors in Scotland, see Nasar Meer, 'Looking up in Scotland? Multinationalism, Multiculturalism and Political Elites', *Ethnic and Racial Studies* 38, no. 9 (2015): 1477–96.

44 Maureen McBride, 'Nationalism and "Sectarianism" in Contemporary Scotland', *Ethnic and Racial Studies* 45, no. 16 (2022): 335–58.

45 Teresa Piacentini, Smina Akhtar, Gareth Mulvey and Ashli Mullen, '"It's Not like It Just Happened That Day": Anti-Racist Solidarity in Two Glasgow Neighbourhoods', in *Social Movements and Everyday Acts of Resistance: Solidarity in a Changing World*, edited by Stamatis Poulakidakos, Anastasia Veneti and Maria Rovisco (New York: Routledge, 2022).

46 Philip Cowley and Dennis Kavanagh, *The British General Election of 2015* (Basingstoke: Palgrave Macmillan, 2015), 310. See also 'How Britain Voted in the 2015 Election' (London: Ipsos MORI, 2019), www.ipsos.com/en-uk/how-britain-voted-2015.

47 Michael Ashcroft, 'How the United Kingdom Voted on Thursday
    ... and Why', Lord Ashcroft Polls, 2016, http://lordashcroftpo
    lls.com/2016/06/how-the-united-kingdom-voted-and-why/.

48 Wyn Jones *et al.*, 'The Dog That Finally Barked', 22, 26; Charlie
    Jeffery, Ailsa Henderson, Roger Scully and Richard Wyn Jones,
    'England's Dissatisfactions and the Conservative Dilemma',
    Political Studies Review 14, no. 3 (2016): 335–48.

49 Matthew J. Goodwin and Oliver Heath, 'The 2016 Referendum,
    Brexit and the Left Behind: An Aggregate-Level Analysis of the
    Result', *The Political Quarterly* 87, no. 3 (2016): 13.

50 Gurminder K. Bhambra, 'Brexit, Trump, and "Methodological
    Whiteness": On the Misrecognition of Race and Class', *The
    British Journal of Sociology* 68, no. S1 (2017): S214–32.

51 The NRS categories are broadly deployed as follows: 'A' refers
    to higher manager, administrative and professional workers; 'B'
    intermediate managerial, administrative and professional; 'C1'
    supervisory, clerical and junior managerial, administrative and
    professional; 'C2' skilled manual workers; 'D' semi-skilled and
    unskilled manual workers; and 'E' state pensioners, casual
    and lowest grade workers, unemployed with state benefits only.

52 Ashcroft, 'How the United Kingdom Voted on Thursday ...
    and Why'.

53 Danny Dorling, 'Brexit: The Decision of a Divided Country',
    BMJ 354, no. 8066 (2016): i3697.

54 Dorling, 'Brexit: The Decision of a Divided Country'.

55 Jonas Marvin has sketched a compelling analysis of the class
    character of the Brexit vote that in some respects aligns with our
    argument above. See Jonas Marvin, 'Brexit From Below: Nation,
    Race and Class', *Salvage* 10 (2021): 53–88.

56 Priska Komaromi and Karissa Singh, 'Post-Referendum
    Racism and Xenophobia: The Role of Social Media Activism
    in Challenging the Normalisation of Xeno-Racist Narratives'
    (London: Institute of Race Relations, 2016), https://irr.org.uk/
    article/post-referendum-racism-and-the-importance-of-social-
    activism/. For a detailed discussion of the place of racism in Brexit
    and its aftermath, see Martin Shaw, *Political Racism: Brexit and
    Its Aftermath* (Newcastle upon Tyne: Agenda Publishing, 2022).

57 The impact of Brexit on the lives of migrants and people
    of colour is extensively discussed in Michaela Benson and

Chantelle Lewis, 'Brexit, British People of Colour in the EU-27 and Everyday Racism in Britain and Europe', *Ethnic and Racial Studies* 42, no. 13 (2019): 2211–28; and Michaela Benson, Nando Sigona, Elena Zambelli and Catherine Craven, 'From the State of the Art to New Directions in Researching What Brexit Means for Migration and Migrants', *Migration Studies* 10, no. 2 (2022). For a discussion of the transnational coloniality in both Brexit and Trump's America, see Ali Meghji, 'Towards a Theoretical Synergy: Critical Race Theory and Decolonial Thought in Trumpamerica and Brexit Britain', *Current Sociology* 70, no. 2 (2020): 647–64.

58 Vron Ware, 'Towards a Sociology of Resentment: A Debate on Class and Whiteness', *Sociological Research Online* 13, no. 5 (2008), www.socresonline.org.uk/13/5/9.html.bak.

59 Steve Fenton, 'Resentment, Class and Social Sentiments about the Nation: The Ethnic Majority in England', *Ethnicities* 12, no. 4 (2012): 465–83.

60 Stuart Hall, 'Interview', in *Rethinking British Decline*, edited by Richard English and Michael Kenny (Basingstoke: Palgrave Macmillan, 2000), 109. Others who identify the spectre of Powell in the Brexit moment include Bhattacharyya *et al.*, *Empire's Endgame*, 65.

61 Theresa May, 'Statement from the New Prime Minister Theresa May', Gov.uk, 2016, www.gov.uk/government/speeches/statement-from-the-new-prime-minister-theresa-may.

62 Kjartan Páll Sveinsson, *Who Cares about the White Working Class?* (London: Runnymede Trust, 2009).

63 Ware, 'Towards a Sociology of Resentment'. On class as a social force, see Edward Palmer Thompson, *The Making of the English Working Class* (London: Penguin, 1991).

64 Emejulu and Bassel, 'Minority Women, Austerity and Activism'.

65 'EU Referendum Results', 2016, www.bbc.co.uk/news/politics/eu_referendum/results.

66 Georgina Sturge, 'General Election 2019: Brexit', House of Commons Library, 2020, https://commonslibrary.parliament.uk/general-election-2019-brexit/.

67 Adam McDonnell and Chris Curtis, 'How Britain Voted in the 2019 General Election' (London: YouGov, 2019), https://yougov.co.uk/topics/politics/articles-reports/2019/12/17/how-britain-voted-2019-general-election.

68 David Cutts, Matthew Goodwin, Oliver Heath and Paula Surridge, 'Brexit, the 2019 General Election and the Realignment of British Politics', *The Political Quarterly* 91, no. 1 (2020): 11–12, DOI: 10.1111/1467-923X.12815.

69 Kenan Malik, 'How We All Colluded in Fortress Europe', *The Guardian*, 10 June 2018, www.theguardian.com/commentis free/2018/jun/10/sunday-essay-how-we-colluded-in-fortress-europe-immigration.

70 For an analysis of the mainstreaming of reactionary populism in Europe, see Mondon and Winter, *Reactionary Democracy*, 147–98.

71 It should be noted here that in the months following the EU referendum, senior Labour Party figures and trade union leaders called for immigration controls from a purportedly left-wing perspective, showing just how widespread the anti-migrant and nationalist moment was in the immediate aftermath of the Brexit vote. See David Bates, '"The Jobs All Go to Foreigners": A Critical Discourse Analysis of the Labour Party's "Left-Wing" Case for Immigration Controls', *Critical Discourse Studies* (2022): 1–17.

72 Featherstone, 'From Out of Apathy to the Post-Political'.

73 Davidson, 'A Scottish Watershed', 21.

Conclusion: amid the ruins

The increasingly entangled web of social inequalities and divisions in Britain today has produced a historic crisis of political representation where the construction of a durable consensus has become almost impossible. Such a profound, multi-level crisis is a symptom of a deeper, systemic malaise that we have tried to historically grasp in this book. First and foremost, its origins lie in the incremental but accelerating erosion of the democratic settlement that once guaranteed unprecedented institutional stability. That settlement consisted of social welfare, voting rights and an electoral vehicle representing the working class. It took a century to construct, and was the convoluted outcome of the emergence of the working class as a social force and the desire of two competing political projects to contain its revolutionary potential. First, there was the imperial nationalism of the Liberal then Conservative blocs. Following them was the socialist nationalism and imperialism of the Labour Party. Despite vying for political power, both blocs held a shared commitment to guaranteeing domestic social order to facilitate the continued expansion of British geopolitical reach and the uninterrupted accumulation of capital. Empire came to play a formative role in both of these competing political projects, preventing the re-emergence of the domestic working class as an insurgent force. This happened in two ways: first, through the partial financing of social welfare and, second, through a racializing imperial British nationalism that ideologically secured their inclusion in the nation in opposition to colonised subjects both at home and abroad. Labour's conception of national belonging was undoubtedly more expansive than that of the Liberals and Conservatives in so far as it sought democratic rights for the majority of the working class still excluded from full social citizenship. However, what unified these two historic blocs was a shared commitment to empire and racialized nationalism as the fundamental cornerstones of domestic stability and social order. The resultant inter-class truce was decisive in maintaining Britain's domination of the modern world-system.

Just as the finishing touches were being put in place to this settlement with the creation of the post-war welfare state, the British empire began to crumble under sustained resistance from the colonised populations of Asia, Africa and the Caribbean. Decolonisation presented the British ruling class with a fundamental conundrum that has stumped it ever since: how to maintain its geopolitical reach and the competitiveness of British capitalism in the aftermath of empire while continuing to deliver the kind of political, economic and psychic security that would guarantee domestic social order? Both the Scottish independence referendum and Brexit are the convoluted artefacts of the failure of the British state to find an answer to this question.

Successive Labour and Conservative governments attempted in vain to stabilise British capitalism through a range of strategies that included the super-exploitation of a racialized reserve army of migrant labour after the war; entry into the European Economic Community in 1973; the neoliberal counter-revolution that crushed the politics and language of class in the 1980s; and the remaking of class as a series of racialized ethnicities under New Labour in the 1990s and 2000s. However, in their efforts to resolve the systemic crisis of British capitalism, these administrations ended up further eroding the basis upon which the historic democratic settlement had rested. One by one, the foundational pillars of this century-long settlement between Britain's ruling elites and its domestic working class have fallen. On the eve of the 2007 financial crash, the process of fragmentation had reached a critical tipping point. With social inequalities widening, the institutional space to articulate working-class grievances was now more diminished than ever due to the obdurate commitment to neoliberalism of the main political parties at Westminster.

When the financial crash hit, the insistence of these parties on the need for austerity directly contributed to a historic crisis of representation and the political vacuum came to be filled by competing nationalist projects in Scotland and England. In Scotland, the working class finally cut its ties to New Labour and moved en masse towards the centre-left nationalist alternative of the SNP which promised to restore elements of the democratic settlement in an independent Scotland. Though the Scottish population voted against independence in 2014 by 55 per cent to 45 per cent, the result revealed a secular decline in support for the union, a decline that continues to this day. The mobilisations for Scottish independence were undergirded by a politics of hope and a desire to construct a political alternative to austerity. In seeking to revive core elements of the post-war welfare state, the movement actually sought to restore a key feature of Britishness, now repackaged for an independent Scotland. And it was the young and middle-aged working-class and middle-class resident in the urban heartlands that constituted the driving force of this new politics in Scotland.

Meanwhile, in England, a political space also opened up for nationalists in the aftermath of the financial crash, but this time it was the reactionary populists of UKIP and the right wing of the Conservative Party that took advantage. For these forces, Britain's problems were the result of its four-decade-long membership of the EU which had incrementally eroded national sovereignty. This was usually highlighted with reference to the EU principle of free movement which, they contended, represented an economic and security threat to Britain. This drift to the right in England would culminate in Brexit in 2016 when Britain voted 52 per cent to 48 per cent to secede from the EU. A sizeable fraction of the working class in England and Wales voted for Brexit as part of a wider cross-class coalition drawn by narratives marbled through with racism which promised to restore economic prosperity if only they were allowed to 'take back control' and stop immigration. Specifically, it was older workers (over the age of 45) and pensioners resident on the periphery of cities or small self-contained towns who were drawn to the politics of Brexit.

What was also striking about the vote for Brexit was how well it aligned with those working-class populations that went down to a series of defeats in the 1980s. The long-standing absence of the politics and language of class resulting from the defeat by neoliberalism has allowed reactionary populists to recast the very real injuries of class into a virulent politics of racist resentment. Real working-class pain – which in a post-imperial state like Britain is necessarily a pain experienced across ethnicities – has come to be understood by substantial numbers of older working people through a racialized lens. This working-class break from the neoliberal settlement is not a sign of an emergent class consciousness, as some on the British left claim, but is instead an indication of its long-term absence. This is most tragically demonstrated by how a part of the working class has been summoned into the camp of the anti-immigrant right which presents the 'white working class' as the main victims of neoliberalism. In actuality, decline and defeat are multi-ethnic processes as we have shown in this book. Further, the idea of a left-behind white working class elides the fact that it is black and brown working-class women who have been disproportionately affected by the dismantling of the democratic settlement.[1]

What these developments highlight is that while Brexit and Scottish independence are both movements of seces-sionism, the constituencies mobilised by them could not be more different. In Scotland, the break with the main political parties has resulted in an uneven shift towards the centre-left terrain previously occupied by Old Labour, whereas in England, the break from neoliberal consensus was initiated by the reactionary populists of the far right. Set against these developments, the long-standing and hitherto durable institutional arrangements of the British state are currently being stretched to their limits. These tensions have already led to Britain seceding from the EU and it is increasingly difficult to see how Scotland and England can be held together in a single unitary state if these contradictory developments deepen further.

We must ask ourselves then what might happen if Britain breaks? For most on the left in Scotland, the British state is understood first and foremost as an imperialist state. As a result, its break-up would be understood as a progressive development, weakening, for example, the capacity of the state to launch imperialist wars as in Iraq in 2003. There is no doubt that Britain without Scotland would have less influence on the global stage, and perhaps attention could be focused more on resolving some of the domestic inequalities and social divisions that scar the contemporary landscape. However, what is often elided by such left discourses is the other, more cosmopolitan and neglected underside of Britain that would be greatly weakened if the state were to break apart.

One of the defining legacies of the entangled anti-racist and class-based social movements of the 1970s was their bifurcation of the white British population, breaking a sizeable minority from the racist consensus that had hitherto held sway. This historic transformation helped prise open a breathing space for everyday multicultures to thrive and flourish over recent decades – not only in urban conurbations,[2] but also increasingly in provincial towns across the country. Ben Rogaly's hopeful portrait of everyday life in Peterborough provides an illustration of such a process, drawing attention to how still-powerful racist impulses now increasingly jostle for space with a consolidating multi-ethnic working-class cosmopolitanism.[3] This is why we have insisted that the

1970s and early 1980s cycle of protest represented a water-shed in British politics, a moment of learning that helped undermine rigid ideas of racialized difference and national belonging. Its long-term effect was to rehumanise Britons of Caribbean and Asian descent and bifurcate the white British population on the question of racism.

While those movements were ultimately defeated as we have shown in this book, they left their traces such that subsequent generations of black and brown Britons encountered a country that was less suffocating, allowing them the space to breathe and sometimes flourish. The complex class structures of Britain's racialized minority communities, particularly the emergence of a black and brown middle class, is just one of the unintended consequences of this legacy.[4] Some of these gains have undoubtedly been rolled back by the years of austerity as new hierarchies of belonging have been generated, targeting migrants and Muslims in particular, while older racisms have been emboldened as demonstrated by the Windrush scandal.[5] At the same time, the imprint of those gains from the 1970s is still traceable in the ease with which many young people handle the lived realities of multi-ethnic life in Britain. This sense of unthinking belonging was denied to the migrant parents and grandparents of black and brown Britons, and we believe it would be a mistake to dismiss the importance of those trenches of hope that have been dug by long-established communities of colour in civil society in an otherwise politically bleak British landscape.

If the departure of Scotland breaks Britain, one possible scenario might be that it will give England the space to finally come to terms with empire and begin to craft a politics worthy of its contemporary multicultural citizenry. However, we believe that would require a viable anti-racist and democratic socialist vehicle in the sphere of institutional politics that could facilitate such a national reckoning and reconciliation. No such vehicle is on the horizon. Instead, in its absence, we believe we would see a strengthening of a reactionary English nationalism, the kind of nationalism that drove the politics of

Brexit. And its first victims would be migrants followed possibly by black and brown Britons.

Contrary, then, to what some – particularly in Scotland – say, the Union Jack is not only the butcher's apron. For many black and brown Britons, identifying with Britishness has provided a sense of belonging in the face of an exclusionary English nationalism.[6] The multi-ethnic composition of England, itself a direct product of empire, has produced contradictory and competing definitions of 'Britishness', not all of which are reducible to the racism of the British state. Of course, this idea of multicultural Britishness can be weaponised by the political right (who played little or no part in its creation). Recent examples of this include the appointment of Priti Patel and then Suella Braverman as Home Secretaries whose primary brief has been to create an increasingly racialized and inhospitable climate for migrants. Nevertheless, the break-up of that state would be accompanied by the unravelling of a fragile multicultural Britishness that was forged in the slipstream of the anti-racist struggles of the 1970s, and that has acted as a bulwark to more exclusionary conceptions of English nationalism up to now. Counterintuitively, those who have been most oppressed and subjugated by the British state now have something to lose by its demise. The left in Scotland who urge the break-up of Britain could be more cognisant of these unintended consequences.

We also have to ask if Scottish independence today would improve the material wellbeing of people in Scotland. After all, it was the failure to find redress for egregious class divisions within the three main British political parties that drove people towards the project of Scottish independence in the first place. There is no doubt that through the efforts of activists in the RIC as well as prominent members of the SNP left like Mhairi Black and others, the 2014 referendum successfully mobilised significant working-class constituencies that had hitherto been bludgeoned into passivity by the three-party cartel of British politics. In this sense, it was a campaign inspired by a politics of hope and which sought to bring questions of class and social inequality to the forefront. However, the radical potential of Scottish independence has faded, in part, because of the strategic failings of the Scottish left and its publics to cohere in a political formation in the immediate aftermath of September 2014. On balance, we can now say that the long-term beneficiary of RIC were not socialists but the SNP. By outcome rather than design, RIC effectively served as an escalator transporting the working class and its allies disillusioned with New Labour into the camp of the SNP, helping to consolidate its hegemony.

This movement of anti-neoliberal sentiment into the SNP posed questions of the party's leadership. Would it assent to the hopes and aspirations of the new membership, widely considered to be to the left of the party elite? We can say that the answer to this question is 'no'. Slowly but assuredly, the radical potential of the new membership has been neutralised as the leadership has increasingly wedded itself to its own form of social neoliberalism.[7] The publication in May 2018 of the Scottish Growth Commission underscored the break from the anti-austerity rhetoric that characterised the 2014 independence movement. The Institute for Fiscal Studies commended the report and what it called the SNP's 'new realism', predicting that it would mean a further ten years of austerity.[8] With independence ever more associated with the SNP, there are no guarantees that a break from the British state will serve as a route towards working-class upliftment.

Further, there is, as we have pointed out, a degree of complacency in the camp of those who advocate for Scottish independence. The desire in Scotland to project onto 'Westminster' everything unsavoury or embarrassing about the union is not only intellectually dishonest but reflects a long-standing unwillingness to confront the enduring legacies of anti-Irish racism and Scotland's disproportionate role in British colonialism. This is traceable in the language of certain elements within the campaign for independence. For example, All Under One Banner, a pressure group that has organised the largest mobilisations for independence since the referendum of

2014, describes Scotland as a 'colony' subjected to the power of 'its imperial masters at Westminster'.[9] Some might dismiss this, but words matter. These formulations betray a Scottish victimhood among parts of the population that stands in the way of any serious reckoning with the past and its ongoing legacies today.[10] Despite recent recognition by SNP politicians of Scotland's role in empire, the gap between elite and popular conceptions on these issues is a further indication of the distance that has yet to be travelled. The prominence of Humza Yousaf and other black and Asian party members in positions of leadership in the SNP is to be welcomed and suggests Scottishness can indeed be imagined as something other than 'white'. In wider society at large, however, these sentiments are far from consolidated, as research has shown.[11] Any subsequent campaigns for Scottish independence will have to prise open these unresolved difficulties.

In fact, when it comes to anti-racism and the politics of class, the resources of hope are arguably greater in England than they are in Scotland. Deposited within sections of the black and brown populations of England are memories of the collective resistance we have discussed in this book. From the workplace strikes against discrimination led by the IWA to the black struggles against state and street racism, it was autonomous collective action that helped turn the tide against systematic discrimination and violence. Collective memories of these cultures of resistance are sedimented in England to a greater degree than in Scotland, although recent popular protests against asylum seeker detentions like that of Kenmure Street indicate the potential for them to be consolidated in Scotland too.

The perennial difficulty since the defeats of the 1980s and the emergence of New Labour in the 1990s is how to find institutional expression for working-class justice in the electoral arrangements of the British state. This is largely due to the three-party cartel and its shared commitment to neoliberalism. Briefly, by chance rather than intention, Jeremy Corbyn was elected leader of the Labour Party in 2015 by a similar demographic to that which turbo-charged the vote for

Scottish independence a year previously. For a brief moment, it appeared that the Labour Party might return to its founding principle of securing social justice for the working class but this time also incorporating demands for racial and sexual justice with an internationalist opposition to imperialist wars. However, it would be crushed by the contradictory class forces driving Brexit, by its failure to grasp the specificity of antisemitism, and by a debilitating faction fight between the left and the majority of the Parliamentary Labour Party.[12] Further, and tellingly, Corbyn's Labour Party failed to revive the party's fortunes in Scotland, where the working class has resolutely attached its mast to that of the SNP. If confirmation were needed that the Labour Party is no longer an electoral vehicle for working-class justice, this was it.

The sociologist Raymond Williams once remarked that '[t]o be truly radical is to make hope possible, rather than despair convincing'.[13] Where, then, might we locate the resources of hope today? The historic juncture facing the left in every part of Britain is whether an expansive political vision can be crafted, one which not only seeks to redress the dehumanising effects of capitalism but in the process allows working people to regain control over their own conditions of life and their relations with one another. Can we close the variance between the increasing lack of material and psychic fulfilment to be found in contemporary society and the desire of ordinary people to live a contented life of happiness and completeness? Potential collective agents against racism and class injustice are not easily identifiable, but a tentative portrait of possibilities can nevertheless be sketched.

While there is no political force currently willing or able to represent it, there exists a social base for a democratic socialist politics. From the Occupy movement to the mobilisations against the Iraq War, and from protests against mounting austerity to the Me Too and Black Lives Matter movements, the demand for class, racial and sexual justice with an internationalist opposition to war has never gone away. This also includes those socialist and green activists who fought for

Scottish independence and who highlighted the need for the left to be more attentive to the uneven development of British capitalism. Alongside them are at least two generations of the so-called precariat. Birthed under neoliberalism, a process of technical class re-composition saw many of the children of the manual working class acquire increasing levels of certi-fied cultural capital yet be ruthlessly pushed into precarious forms of employment. This new working class ranges from those working all hours in the so-called gig economy to that growing army of younger professionals in sectors such as higher education increasingly subject to the full force of proletarianisation.

Hope might also be found in a more everyday sense in the very fact of contemporary multi-ethnic life in Britain. We are, to put it simply, much more entangled in each other's lives than was once the case. Nearly one in ten people in England and Wales are involved in so-called mixed relationships, and nearly half of these are with someone from the majority 'white' population.[14] The retreat of col-lectivism that has come to define the neoliberal era has also been accompanied by the emergence of a fragile but dis-cernible everyday multicultural reality, particularly among younger generations.

One of the key lessons to be learned from the anti-systemic struggles of the 1970s was how the cross-pollination of resistance produced a solidarity that in turn helped erode one of the principal ideological ballasts of modern capitalist rule – the hierarchical ordering of difference.[15] Despite the bleakness of the overall picture, it may, conversely, prove to be easier to construct such solidarity today because of the achievements of those anti-systemic movements of the now distant past. For example, what W.E.B. Du Bois referred to as the 'wages of whiteness' no longer deliver the scale of material advantage they once did.[16] And although racism continues to shape class experience, the structural and symbolic conditions of existence facing the white, black and brown working class are more similar than they have ever been in British history.

There is therefore an opportunity to prise open the cracks in the system of domination and no longer remain indifferent to the suffering of fellow humans. Only by opening up such alternative ways of imagining life can dignity and freedom be delivered to all.

Significantly, this moment has arisen at a time when the ruling elites are internally divided and arguably rudderless. The Conservative Party, having absorbed the two contradictory blocs that drove Brexit, is now being torn apart by those same currents pulling in different directions in the context of soaring inflation and a cost of living crisis that has pushed the British economy into recession and large parts of its population into penury. When Liz Truss succeeded Boris Johnson as Prime Minister, her efforts, and that of her Chancellor, Kwasi Kwarteng, to kick-start a long-stagnating economy through unfunded tax cuts and public borrowing sparked unprecedented fear in the global markets leaving the project still-born and in ruins. And with it has gone the credibility of the Conservative government. This is the context in which Rishi Sunak ascended to the office of Prime Minister to present, alongside his Chancellor, Jeremy Hunt, a more familiar Conservative vision: a continuation of declining living standards today and eye-watering austerity tomorrow. The government's own Office for Budget Responsibility forecasts UK household incomes will fall by more than 7 per cent by 2024 – the biggest decline since records began. As we have shown in this book, the opportunities generated by such turbulence have generally been seized by the hard right, but it need not be so.

It was the lowest of the low in the hierarchy of labour that established the ILP and then the Labour Party to redress the social inequalities of a previous age. Can there be an equivalent emergence today? It seems clear that the election of a Labour government led by Keir Starmer will not alleviate the multi-level crisis we have described. Put simply: it will not deliver social justice to the working class. In opposition, it has already committed itself to a set of self-imposed fiscal rules such as borrowing only to invest that will strictly limit its ability to arrest growing social inequalities.[17] Further, in a disturbing echo of Gordon Brown's infamous call for 'British jobs for British workers', Starmer has insisted that the British economy must wean itself off its reliance on migrant labour. Instead, his alternative to fill the resulting shortage of labour seeks to discipline the poor, the disabled and those caring for elderly relatives and force them back into the labour market.[18] Further, his refusal to back striking workers across a range of sectors ominously signals what is likely to come in the event of Labour returning to power.

There is a real danger of being disappointed, then, if our sole means of redress is limited to the election of a Labour government. This is why it is of the utmost importance that the multifarious social movements and emergent working-class collective action maintain their autonomy from the Labour Party. We believe now is the time for the contemporary working class and its allies to demand social justice and freedom from the degrading logic of a capitalism in permanent crisis. Class, to quote Edward Thompson, is not just a category but 'something which in fact happens (and can be shown to have happened) in human relationships'.[19] For these emergent cultures of resistance to cohere politically, class will have to happen.

And there are some grounds for cautious optimism. When tens of thousands of rail workers took industrial action to arrest the accelerating decline in living standards and the Conservative destruction of public services, they set in motion a wave of workers' militancy not witnessed in Britain for a generation. They were soon joined by nurses, school teachers, those working in higher education, British Telecom and Royal Mail postal workers, with more sectors still to follow. While this sort of collective action remains largely defensive, seeking to protect labouring people from a further diminution in their living standards, it has the potential, if sustained, to transform political consciousness. It is only through such a process of collective self-awakening that the multi-ethnic working class will acquire the capacity to secure meaningful upliftment, be it the demand for political and economic justice or effective opposition to racism and gendered inequality. If democratic structures of dissent can be manufactured, there is a possibility that the language of class and socialism can be regenerated for the twenty-first century underpinned by visions of an alternative society – one based on justice and need, not greed and profit. If the unrepresented assemblages discussed in this book can, against the odds, find new and creative ways of building solidarities amid the ruins, the working class can be remade once again as a social force. This is the route out of permanent crisis and fragmentation. If it is found, this new working class – black, brown, white and migrant – will start to make its own history.

Notes

1 Emejulu and Bassel, 'Minority Women, Austerity and Activism'. See also Hall *et al.*, 'Intersecting Inequalities'.
2 See, for example, Emma Jackson, 'Valuing the Bowling Alley: Contestations over the Preservation of Spaces of Everyday Urban Multiculture in London', *The Sociological Review* 67, no. 1 (2019): 79–94; Sivamohan Valluvan, 'Conviviality and Multiculture: A Post-Integration Sociology of Multi-Ethnic Interaction', *YOUNG* 24, no. 3 (2016): 204–21.
3 Ben Rogaly, *Stories from a Migrant City: Living and Working Together in the Shadow of Brexit* (Manchester: Manchester University Press, 2020).
4 Satnam Virdee, '"Race", Employment and Social Change: A Critique of Current Orthodoxies', *Ethnic and Racial Studies* 29, no. 4 (2006): 605–28.
5 Les Back and Shamser Sinha, *Migrant City* (London: Routledge, 2019). Luke de Noronha, *Deporting Black Britons: Portraits of Deportation to Jamaica* (Manchester: Manchester University Press, 2020). Nadya Ali and Ben Whitham, 'Racial Capitalism, Islamophobia and Austerity', *International Political Sociology* 15, no. 2 (2021): 190–211.

6   Stephen Jivraj, 'Who Feels British? The Relationship Between
    Ethnicity, Religion and National Identity in England', Dynamics
    of Diversity: Evidence from the 2011 Census (Manchester: Centre
    on Dynamics of Ethnicity, 2013), https://hummedia.manchester.
    ac.uk/institutes/code/briefingsupdated/who-feels-british.pdf.

7   Dave Featherstone, Lazaros Karaliotas, Neil Davidson, Satnam
    Virdee, Jenny Morrison and Gerry Mooney, 'Scotland and
    Alternatives to Neoliberalism: Roundtable Discussion with Neil
    Davidson, Satnam Virdee, Jenny Morrison and Gerry Mooney',
    Soundings 1, no. 63 (2016): 55–73. See also Gallagher *et al.*,
    Roch Winds.

8   Featherstone, 'From Out of Apathy to the Post-Political', 485.
    See also Foley, 'Europeanisation, Devolution and Popular
    Sovereignty', 453–54.

9   See https://twitter.com/AUOBNOW/status/1329038351131873
    280 and www.dailyrecord.co.uk/news/politics/snp-msp-faces-
    online-abuse-23379754.

10 On empire and Scottish victimhood, see Stephen Howe, 'Anti-
    Colonialism in Twentieth-Century Scotland', in *Scotland, Empire,
    and Decolonisation in the Twentieth Century*, edited by Bryan
    Glass and John MacKenzie (Manchester: Manchester University
    Press, 2015).

11 Satnam Virdee, Christopher Kyriakides and Tariq Modood,
    'Codes of Cultural Belonging: Racialised National Identities in
    a Multi-Ethnic Scottish Neighbourhood', *Sociological Research
    Online* 11, no. 4 (2006), www.socresonline.org.uk/11/4/virdee.
    html.

12 For an overview of Labour and antisemitism during the Corbyn
    period, see Ben Gidley, Brendan McGeever and David Feldman,
    'Labour and Antisemitism: A Crisis Misunderstood', *The Political
    Quarterly* 91, no. 2 (2020): 413–21.

13 Raymond Williams, *Resources of Hope: Culture, Democracy,
    Socialism* (London: Verso Books, 1989), 118.

14 'What Does The 2011 Census Tell Us About Inter-Ethnic
    Relationships?', 2011 Census Analysis (London: Office for
    National Statistics, 2011), www.ons.gov.uk/peoplepopulationan
    dcommunity/birthsdeathsandmarriages/marriagecohabitation
    andcivilpartnerships/articles/whatdoesthe2011censustellusab
    outinterethnicrelationships/2014-07-03.

15 Some of these criss-crossing solidarities can also be evidenced as late as the mid-1980s during the miners' strike. See, for example, Diarmaid Kelliher, *Making Cultures of Solidarity: London and the 1984–5 Miners' Strike* (New York: Routledge, 2021).

16 W.E.B. Du Bois, *Black Reconstruction in America, 1860–1880* (New York: The Free Press, 1998). John Narayan, 'The Wages of Whiteness in the Absence of Wages: Racial Capitalism, Reactionary Intercommunalism and the Rise of Trumpism', *Third World Quarterly* 38, no. 11 (2017): 2482–500.

17 Richard Partington, 'Labour to Pledge "Ironclad Discipline" with Public Finances', *The Guardian*, 12 July 2022.

18 Jessica Elgot, 'Keir Starmer Vows to Wean Business off "Cheap Labour"', *The Guardian*, 22 November 2022.

19 Thompson, *The Making of the English Working Class*, 8.

Bibliography

'30 Years of British Social Attitudes Self-Reported Racial Prejudice Data'. London: NatCen Social Research, 2014. www.bsa.natcen. ac.uk/media/38110/selfreported-racial-prejudice-datafinal.pdf.

Ali, Nadya, and Ben Whitham, 'Racial Capitalism, Islamophobia and Austerity', *International Political Sociology* 15, no. 2 (2021): 190–211.

Alston, David. *Slaves and Highlanders: Silenced Histories of Scotland and the Caribbean*. Edinburgh: Edinburgh University Press, 2021.

Anderson, Perry. 'Origins of the Present Crisis'. *New Left Review* 1, no. 23 (1964): 26–53.

Anderson, Perry. 'Ukania Perpetua?' *New Left Review* 125 (2020): 35–107.

'Anti-Social Behaviour Order Statistics: England and Wales 2013 Key Findings'. London: Gov.uk, 2014. www.gov.uk/govern ment/statistics/anti-social-behaviour-order-statistics-england-and-wales-2013/anti-social-behaviour-order-statistics-england-and-wales-2013-key-findings.

Ashcroft, Michael. 'How the United Kingdom Voted on Thursday ... and Why'. Lord Ashcroft Polls, 2016. http://lordashcroftpolls. com/2016/06/how-the-united-kingdom-voted-and-why/.

Ashe, Stephen, Satnam Virdee and Laurence Brown. 'Striking Back against Racist Violence in the East End of London, 1968–1970'. *Race & Class* 58, no. 1 (2016): 34–54.

Audickas, Lukas, Noel Dempsey and Philip Loft. 'Membership of UK Political Parties'. House of Commons Library, 2019. https:// commonslibrary.parliament.uk/research-briefings/sn05125/.

Back, Les and Shamser Sinha. *Migrant City*. London: Routledge, 2019.

Back, Les, Michael Keith, Azra Khan, Kalbir Shukra and John
    Solomos. 'New Labour's White Heart: Politics, Multiculturalism
    and the Return of Assimilation'. *The Political Quarterly* 73,
    no. 4 (2002): 445–54. DOI: 10.1111/1467-923X.00499.

Baldwin, Lewis V., Amiri YaSin Al-Hadid, Stephen W. Angell and
    Anthony B. Pinn. *Between Cross and Crescent: Christian
    and Muslim Perspectives on Malcolm and Martin*. Gainesville:
    University Press of Florida, 2002.

Bates, David. '"The Jobs All Go to Foreigners": A Critical Discourse
    Analysis of the Labour Party's "Left-Wing" Case for Immigration
    Controls'. *Critical Discourse Studies* (2022): 1–17.

BBC News. 'Full Text: Blair on Law and Order'. 2004. http://news.
    bbc.co.uk/1/hi/uk_politics/3907651.stm.

Belchem, John. 'English Working-Class Radicalism and the Irish,
    1815–50'. In *The Irish in the Victorian City*, edited by Roger
    Swift and Sheridan Gilley, 85–97. London: Routledge, 1985.

Benson, Michaela and Chantelle Lewis. 'Brexit, British People
    of Colour in the EU-27 and Everyday Racism in Britain and
    Europe'. *Ethnic and Racial Studies* 42, no. 13 (2019): 2211–28.

Benson, Michaela, Nando Sigona, Elena Zambelli and Catherine
    Craven. 'From the State of the Art to New Directions in
    Researching What Brexit Means for Migration and Migrants'.
    Migration Studies 10, no. 2 (2022): 374–90.

Bhambra, Gurminder K. 'Brexit, Trump, and "Methodological
    Whiteness": On the Misrecognition of Race and Class'. *The
    British Journal of Sociology* 68, no. S1 (2017): S214–32.

Bhambra, Gurminder K. 'Locating Brexit in the Pragmatics of Race,
    Citizenship and Empire'. In *Brexit: Sociological Responses*, edited
    by William Outhwaite, 91–99. London: Anthem Press, 2017.

Bhambra, Gurminder K. 'Relations of Extraction, Relations of
    Redistribution: Empire, Nation, and the Construction of the
    British Welfare State'. *The British Journal of Sociology* 73,
    no. 1 (2022): 4–15.

Bhattacharyya, Gargi, Adam Elliott-Cooper, Sita Balani, Kerem
    Nisancioglu, Kojo Koram and Dalia Gebrial. *Empire's
    Endgame: Racism and the British State*. London: Pluto Press,
    2021.

Birchall, Ian H. *The Smallest Mass Party in the World: Building
    the Socialist Workers Party, 1951–1979*. London: Socialists
    Unlimited, 1981.

Blair, Tony. 'Forging a New Agenda'. *Marxism Today*, October (1991): 32–34.

Blair, Tony. 'The Callaghan Memorial Lecture'. Cardiff City Hall, 2007. http://image.guardian.co.uk/sys-files/Politics/documents/2007/04/11/blairlecture.pdf.

Blair, Tony. 'Tony Blair: "My Job Was to Build on Some Thatcher Policies"'. *BBC News*, 2013. www.bbc.co.uk/news/av/uk-politics-22073434.

Blair, Tony and Gerhard Schroeder. *Europe: The Third Way/Die Neue Mitte*. Johannesburg: Friedrich Ebert Foundation South Africa Office, 1998.

Bonnett, Alastair. *White Identities: An Historical & International Introduction*. London: Routledge, 1999.

Bowser, Benjamin P., Louis Kushnick and Paul Grant. 'Catching History on the Wing: A. Sivanandan as Activist, Teacher and Rebel'. In *Against the Odds: Scholars Who Challenged Racism in the Twentieth Century*, edited by Benjamin P. Bowser, Louis Kushnick and Paul Grant, 227–42. Amherst, MA: University of Massachusetts Press, 2004.

Brown, Gordon. 'The Politics of Potential: A New Agenda for Labour'. In *Reinventing the Left*, edited by David Miliband. Cambridge: Polity Press, 1994.

Burkett, Jodi. *Constructing Post-Imperial Britain: Britishness, 'Race' and the Radical Left in the 1960s*. Basingstoke: Palgrave Macmillan, 2013.

Burns, Conor. 'Margaret Thatcher's Greatest Achievement: New Labour'. CentreRight, 2008. https://conservativehome.blogs.com/centreright/2008/04/making-history.html.

Butler, David and Dennis Kavanagh. *The British General Election of 1979*. Basingstoke: Palgrave Macmillan, 1980.

Butler, David and Dennis Kavanagh. *The British General Election of 1983*. Basingstoke: Palgrave Macmillan, 1985.

Butler, David and Dennis Kavanagh. *The British General Election of 1987*. Basingstoke: Palgrave Macmillan, 1988.

Butler, David and Dennis Kavanagh. *The British General Election of 1992*. Basingstoke: Palgrave Macmillan, 1993.

Butler, David and Dennis Kavanagh. *The British General Election of 1997*. Basingstoke: Palgrave Macmillan, 1997.

Carter, Bob, Clive Harris and Shirley Joshi. 'The 1951–55 Conservative Government and the Racialization of Black Immigration'. *Immigrants & Minorities* 6, no. 3 (1987): 335–47.

The City of Edinburgh Council. 'Edinburgh Slavery and Colonialism Legacy Review', 2021. www.edinburgh.gov.uk/edinburghsla verycolonialism.

Colley, Linda. *Britons: Forging the Nation, 1707–1837*. London: Vintage, 1996.

Conley, Hazel. 'Economic Crisis, Austerity and Gender Equality: The UK Case'. *European Gender Equality Law Review* 2 (2012): 14–19.

Conley, Hazel. 'Using Equality to Challenge Austerity: New Actors, Old Problems'. *Work, Employment and Society* 26, no. 2 (1 April 2012): 349–59. DOI: 10.1177/0950017011432906.

Cowley, Philip and Dennis Kavanagh. *The British General Election of 2010*. Basingstoke: Palgrave Macmillan, 2010.

Cowley, Philip and Dennis Kavanagh. *The British General Election of 2015*. Basingstoke: Palgrave Macmillan, 2015.

Crown Office and Procurator Fiscal Service. 'Hate Crime in Scotland 2020–21'. Edinburgh, 2021. www.copfs.gov.uk/about-copfs/ news/hate-crime-in-scotland-2020-21/.

Curtis, L. Perry. *Anglo-Saxons and Celts: A Study of Anti-Irish Prejudice in Victorian England*. New York: New York University Press, 1968.

Cutts, David, Matthew Goodwin, Oliver Heath and Paula Surridge. 'Brexit, the 2019 General Election and the Realignment of British Politics'. *The Political Quarterly* 91, no. 1 (2020): 7–23. DOI: 10.1111/1467-923X.12815.

Daniel, William Wentworth. *Racial Discrimination in England*. London: Penguin Books, 1968.

Darlington, Ralph. *The Dynamics of Workplace Unionism: Shop Stewards' Organization in Three Merseyside Plants*. First Edition. London: Thomson Learning, 1994.

Davidson, Neil. 'The Neoliberal Era in Britain: Historical Developments and Current Perspectives'. *International Socialism* 139 (2013). http://isj.org.uk/the-neoliberal-era-in-britain-historical-developments-and-current-perspectives/.

Davidson, Neil. 'Neoliberal Politics in a Devolved Scotland'. In *NeoLiberal Scotland: Class and Society in a Stateless Nation*, edited by Neil Davidson, Patricia McCafferty and David Miller, 171–223. Newcastle: Cambridge Scholars Publishing, 2010.

Davidson, Neil. 'The New Middle Class and the Changing Social Base of Neoliberalism: A First Approximation'. *The Oxford*

Left Review (blog), 2015. https://oxfordleftreview.com/olr-issue-14/niel-davidson-the-new-middle-class-and-the-changing-social-base-of-neoliberalism-a-first-approximation/.

Davidson, Neil. 'A Scottish Watershed'. *New Left Review* 1, no. 89 (2014): 5–26.

Davidson, Neil. 'What Was Neoliberalism?' In *NeoLiberal Scotland: Class and Society in a Stateless Nation*, edited by Neil Davidson, Patricia McCafferty and David Miller, 1–89. Newcastle: Cambridge Scholars Publishing, 2010.

Deeming, Christopher. 'Foundations of the Workfare State: Reflections on the Political Transformation of the Welfare State in Britain'. *Social Policy & Administration* 49, no. 7 (2015): 862–86.

Devine, Tom. *The Scottish Nation: 1700–2007*. London: Penguin, 2006.

Disraeli, Benjamin. 'Parliamentary Reform – Representation of the People Bill – [Bill 237] – Third Reading (Hansard, 15 July 1867)'. 1867. https://api.parliament.uk/historic-hansard/commons/1867/jul/15/parliamentary-reform-representation-of#S3V0188P0_1867 0715_HOC_87.

Disraeli, Benjamin. 'Parliamentary Reform – Representation of the People Bill – Leave, First Reading (Hansard, 18 March 1867)'. 1867. https://api.parliament.uk/historic-hansard/commons/1867/mar/18/leave-first-reading#S3V0186P0_18670318_HOC_30.

Dixon, David. 'Thatcher's People: The British Nationality Act 1981'. *Journal of Law and Society* 10, no. 2 (1983): 161–80.

Dorling, Danny. 'Brexit: The Decision of a Divided Country'. *BMJ* 354, no. 8066 (2016): i3697.

Du Bois, W.E.B. *Black Reconstruction in America 1860–1880*. New York: The Free Press, 1998.

Duffield, Mark R. *Black Radicalism and the Politics of Deindustrialization: The Hidden History of Indian Foundry Workers in the West Midlands*. Aldershot: Avebury, 1988.

Edgerton, David. *The Rise and Fall of the British Nation: A Twentieth-Century History*. London: Penguin, 2019.

Eldridge, John, Peter Cressey and John MacInnes. *Industrial Sociology and Economic Crisis*. New York: Harvester Wheatsheaf, 1991.

El-Enany, Nadine. *Bordering Britain: Law, Race and Empire*. Manchester: Manchester University Press, 2020.

Elgot, Jessica. 'Keir Starmer Vows to Wean Business off "Cheap Labour"'. *The Guardian*, 22 November 2022.

Emejulu, Akwugo and Leah Bassel. 'Austerity and the Politics of Becoming'. *Journal of Common Market Studies* 56, no. S1 (2018): 109–19. DOI: 10.1111/jcms.12774.

Emejulu, Akwugo and Leah Bassel. 'Minority Women, Austerity and Activism'. *Race & Class* 57, no. 2 (1 October 2015): 86–95. DOI: 10.1177/0306396815595913.

'EU Referendum Results'. 2016. www.bbc.co.uk/news/politics/eu_referendum/results.

Featherstone, Dave, Lazaros Karaliotas, Neil Davidson, Satnam Virdee, Jenny Morrison and Gerry Mooney. 'Scotland and Alternatives to Neoliberalism: Roundtable Discussion with Neil Davidson, Satnam Virdee, Jenny Morrison and Gerry Mooney'. *Soundings* 1, no. 63 (2016): 55–73.

Featherstone, David. 'From Out of Apathy to the Post-Political: The Spatial Politics of Austerity, the Geographies of Politicisation and the Trajectories of the Scottish Left(s)'. *Environment and Planning C: Politics and Space* 39, no. 3 (2021): 469–90.

Featherstone, David. 'Revolt on Clydeside? Space, Politics and Populism'. *Geoforum* 62 (2015): 193–95.

Featherstone, David. *Solidarity: Hidden Histories and Geographies of Internationalism*. London: Zed Books, 2012.

Fenton, Steve. 'Resentment, Class and Social Sentiments about the Nation: The Ethnic Majority in England'. *Ethnicities* 12, no. 4 (2012): 465–83.

Finlayson, Alan. *Making Sense of New Labour*. London: Lawrence & Wishart, 2003.

Fisher, Mark. 'The Occupied Times: Good For Nothing'. *The Occupied Times* (blog), 2014. https://theoccupiedtimes.org/?p=12841.

Fishman, Nina. 'No Home but the Trade Union Movement'. In *Opening the Books: Essays on the Social and Cultural History of British Communist Party*, edited by Geoff Andrews, Nina Fishman and Kevin Morgan. London: Pluto Press, 1995.

Fishman, William J. *East End Jewish Radicals 1875–1914*. Nottingham: Five Leaves Publications, 2004.

Foley, James. 'Europeanisation, Devolution and Popular Sovereignty: On the Politics of State Transformation in Scottish Nationalism'. *Critical Sociology* 48, no. 3 (2022): 437–58.

Gallagher, Cailean, Amy Westwell and Rory Scothorne. *Roch Winds: A Treacherous Guide to the State of Scotland.* Edinburgh: Luath Press Ltd, 2016.

Gamble, Andrew. *Britain in Decline: Economic Policy, Political Strategy and the British State.* London: Macmillan Education, 1994.

Gibbs, Ewan. *Coal Country: The Meaning and Memory of Deindustrialization in Postwar Scotland.* London: University of London Press, 2021.

Giddens, Anthony. *The Third Way: The Renewal of Social Democracy.* Malden: Polity, 1998.

Gidley, Ben, Brendan McGeever and David Feldman. 'Labour and Antisemitism: A Crisis Misunderstood'. *The Political Quarterly* 91, no. 2 (2020): 413–21.

Gilligan, Chris. 'Methodological Nationalism and the Northern Ireland Blind-Spot in Ethnic and Racial Studies'. *Ethnic and Racial Studies* (3 August 2021): 1–21. DOI: 10.1080/01419870.2021.1950793.

Gilligan, Chris. *Northern Ireland and the Crisis of Anti-Racism: Rethinking Racism and Sectarianism.* Manchester: Manchester University Press, 2017.

Gilmour, Ian Hedworth John Little. *Inside Right: A Study of Conservatism.* London: Hutchinson, 1977.

Gilroy, Paul. *There Ain't No Black in the Union Jack.* London: Routledge, 1987.

Glass, Bryan. *The Scottish Nation at Empire's End.* Basingstoke: Palgrave Macmillan, 2014.

Glass, Bryan and John M. MacKenzie, eds. *Scotland, Empire and Decolonisation in the Twentieth Century.* Manchester: Manchester University Press, 2015.

Goodfellow, Maya. *Hostile Environment: How Immigrants Became Scapegoats.* London: Verso Books, 2019.

Goodwin, Matthew J. and Oliver Heath. 'The 2016 Referendum, Brexit and the Left Behind: An Aggregate-Level Analysis of the Result'. *The Political Quarterly* 87, no. 3 (2016): 323–32.

Gopal, Priyamvada. *Insurgent Empire: Anticolonial Resistance and British Dissent.* London: Verso Books, 2020.

Gould, Philip. *The Unfinished Revolution: How the Modernisers Saved the Labour Party.* London: Little, Brown & Company, 1998.

Gramsci, Antonio. *Selections from the Prison Notebooks*. Edited by Quintin Hoare and Geoffrey Nowell-Smith. London: Lawrence & Wishart, 1971.

Gray, Ben. 'Ben Tillett and the Rise of the Labour Movement in Britain'. *History Review* 34 (1999).

Grint, Keith. *The Sociology of Work: An Introduction*. Cambridge: Polity Press, 1991.

Gupta, Partha Sarathi. *Imperialism and the British Labour Movement, 1914–1964*. New York: Holmes and Meier Publishers, 1975.

Hall, Catherine. 'Rethinking Imperial Histories: The Reform Act of 1867'. *New Left Review* 1, no. 208 (1994): 3–29.

Hall, Sarah-Marie, Kimberly McIntosh, Eva Neitzert, Laura Pottinger, K. Sandhu, Mary-Ann Stephenson, Howard Reed and Leonie Taylor. 'Intersecting Inequalities: The Impact of Austerity on Black and Minority Ethnic Women in the UK'. London: Runnymede Trust, Women's Budget Group with RECLAIM and Coventry Women's Voices, 2017. https://wbg.org.uk/wp-content/uploads/2018/08/Intersecting-Inequalities-October-2017-Full-Report.pdf.

Hall, Stuart. 'Interview'. In *Rethinking British Decline*, edited by Richard English and Michael Kenny, 106–16. Basingstoke: Palgrave Macmillan, 2000.

Hall, Stuart. 'New Labour's Double-Shuffle'. *Review of Education, Pedagogy, and Cultural Studies* 27, no. 4 (2005): 319–35.

Hall, Stuart. 'The Great Moving Right Show'. *Marxism Today*, January (1979): 14–20.

Hall, Stuart, and Martin Jacques, eds. *New Times: The Changing Face of Politics in the 1990s*. London: Lawrence & Wishart, 1989.

Hall, Stuart, Chas Critcher, Tony Jefferson, John Clarke and Brian Roberts. *Policing the Crisis: Mugging, the State and Law and Order*. London: Macmillan, 1978.

Hancox, Alfie. 'Alfie Hancox: The Imperialist Soul of Social Democrats'. *The Elephant* (blog), 16 July 2021. www.theelephant.info/ideas/2021/07/16/the-imperialist-soul-of-social-democrats/.

Harvey, David. *The Condition of Postmodernity: An Enquiry into the Origins of Cultural Change*. Oxford: Wiley-Blackwell, 1991.

Hastings, Annette, and Maria Gannon. 'Frontline Public Sector Workers Acted as "Shock Absorbers" of the Austerity Cuts to

Local Government Budgets'. *LSE British Politics and Policy* (blog), 2021. https://blogs.lse.ac.uk/politicsandpolicy/frontline-public-sector-workers-austerity/.

Hay, James Roy. *The Origins of the Liberal Welfare Reforms: 1906–1914*. London: Macmillan Education, 1987.

Haylett, Chris. 'Illegitimate Subjects? Abject Whites, Neoliberal Modernisation, and Middle-Class Multiculturalism'. *Environment and Planning D: Society and Space* 19, no. 3 (2001): 351–70.

Hayton, Richard. 'The UK Independence Party and the Politics of Englishness'. *Political Studies Review* 14, no. 3 (2016): 400–10.

Hearn, Jonathan S. *Claiming Scotland: National Identity and Liberal Culture*. Edinburgh: Polygon at Edinburgh University Press, 2000.

Heffer, Simon. *Like the Roman: The Life of Enoch Powell by Simon Heffer*. 2nd Edition. London: Weidenfeld & Nicolson, 1998.

Heller, Henry. *The Birth of Capitalism: A 21st Century Perspective – the Future of World Capitalism*. London: Pluto Press, 2011.

Hennessy, Peter. *The Prime Minister: The Office and its Holders Since 1945*. London: Penguin, 2001.

Hill, Amelia. 'Racism Is Institutional in Upper Tiers of British Society, Says Lord Parekh'. *The Guardian*, 22 November 2010. www.theguardian.com/world/2010/nov/22/racism-institutional-british-society-report-parekh.

Hill, Amelia. 'UK Life Expectancy Improvement Has Stalled, Figures Show'. *The Guardian*, 25 September 2018. www.theguardian.com/science/2018/sep/25/improvement-uk-life-expectancy-stalled-ons-figures-show.

Hilson, Mary. 'Women Voters and the Rhetoric of Patriotism in the British General Election of 1918'. *Women's History Review* 10, no. 2 (2001): 325–47.

Hinds, Allister. 'Sterling and Decolonization in the British Empire, 1945–1958'. *Social and Economic Studies* 48, no. 4 (1999): 97–116.

Hinton, James and Richard Hyman. *Trade Unions and Revolution: The Industrial Politics of the Early British Communist Party*. London: Pluto Press, 1975.

Hirsch, Shirin. *In the Shadow of Enoch Powell: Race, Locality and Resistance*. Manchester: Manchester University Press, 2018.

Hirshfield, Claire. 'The British Left and the "Jewish Conspiracy": A Case Study of Modern Antisemitism'. *Jewish Social Studies* 43, no. 2 (1981): 95–112.

Hobsbawm, Eric J. *The Age of Capital 1848–1875*. London: Abacus, 1997.

Hobsbawm, Eric J. *Industry and Empire: From 1750 to the Present Day*. London: Penguin, 1990.

Hobsbawm, Eric J. 'Trade Union History'. *The Economic History Review* 20, no. 2 (1967): 358–64.

Horsman, Reginald. 'Origins of Racial Anglo-Saxonism in Great Britain Before 1850'. *Journal of the History of Ideas* 37, no. 3 (1976): 387–410.

'How Britain Voted in the 2015 Election'. London: Ipsos MORI, 2019. www.ipsos.com/en-uk/how-britain-voted-2015.

Howe, Stephen. 'Anti-Colonialism in Twentieth-Century Scotland'. In *Scotland, Empire, and Decolonisation in the Twentieth Century*, edited by Bryan Glass and John MacKenzie, 113–30. Manchester: Manchester University Press, 2015.

Inikori, Joseph E. *Africans and the Industrial Revolution in England: A Study in International Trade and Economic Development*. Cambridge: Cambridge University Press, 2002.

Jackson, Ben. *The Case for Scottish Independence: A History of Nationalist Political Thought in Scotland*. Cambridge: Cambridge University Press, 2020.

Jackson, Emma. 'Valuing the Bowling Alley: Contestations over the Preservation of Spaces of Everyday Urban Multiculture in London'. *The Sociological Review* 67, no. 1 (2019): 79–94.

James, Cyril Lionel Robert. *The Black Jacobins: Toussaint L'ouverture and the San Domingo Revolution*. London: Penguin, 2001.

Jeffery, Charlie, Ailsa Henderson, Roger Scully and Richard Wyn Jones. 'England's Dissatisfactions and the Conservative Dilemma'. *Political Studies Review* 14, no. 3 (2016): 335–48.

Jessop, Bob. 'Authoritarian Neoliberalism: Periodization and Critique'. *South Atlantic Quarterly* 118, no. 2 (2019): 343–61.

Jessop, Bob. 'The Capitalist State and the Rule of Capital: Problems in the Analysis of Business Associations'. *West European Politics* 6, no. 2 (1983): 139–62.

Jessop, Bob. 'From Thatcherism to New Labour: Neo-Liberalism, Workfarism and Labour-Market Regulation'. In *The Political*

Economy of European Employment: European Integration and the Transnationalization of the (Un)Employment Question, edited by Henk Overbeek, 137–53. London: Routledge, 2003.

Jivraj, Stephen. 'Who Feels British? The Relationship Between Ethnicity, Religion and National Identity in England'. *Dynamics of Diversity: Evidence from the 2011 Census*. Manchester: Centre on Dynamics of Ethnicity, 2013. https://hummedia.manchester.ac.uk/institutes/code/briefingsupdated/who-feels-british.pdf.

Johnson, Paul. 'Spending Review 2013: Opening Remarks', 27 June 2013. https://ifs.org.uk/publications/6775.

Josephides, S. 'Principles, Strategies and Anti-Racist Campaigns'. In *Black Politics in Britain*, edited by Harry Goulbourne. Aldershot: Avebury, 1990.

Joyce, Robert, and Xiaowei Xu. 'Inequalities in the Twenty-First Century: Introducing the IFS Deaton Review'. The Institute for Fiscal Studies, 2019. https://ifs.org.uk/inequality/chapter/briefing-note/.

Kelliher, Diarmaid. *Making Cultures of Solidarity: London and the 1984–5 Miners' Strike*. New York: Routledge, 2021.

Kelly, John E. *Trade Unions and Socialist Politics*. London: Verso Books, 1988.

Kessler, Sidney, and Frederic Joseph Bayliss. *Contemporary British Industrial Relations*. London: Macmillan Business, 1995.

Khachaturian, Rafael. 'The Loss of Nicos Poulantzas: The Elusive Answer'. *The Loss of Nicos Poulantzas: The Elusive Answer* (blog), 2017. www.versobooks.com/blogs/3525-the-loss-of-nicos-poulantzas-the-elusive-answer.

Kiely, Ray. *The Neoliberal Paradox*. Cheltenham: Edward Elgar, 2018. DOI: 10.4337/9781788114424.

Knox, William. 'Religion and the Scottish Labour Movement, c.1900–1939'. *Journal of Contemporary History* 23, no. 4 (1988): 609–30.

Komaromi, Priska and Karissa Singh. 'Post-Referendum Racism and Xenophobia: The Role of Social Media Activism in Challenging the Normalisation of Xeno-Racist Narratives'. London: Institute of Race Relations, 2016. https://irr.org.uk/article/post-referendum-racism-and-the-importance-of-social-activism/.

Koram, Kojo. *Uncommon Wealth: Britain and the Aftermath of Empire*. London: John Murray, 2022.

Kundnani, Arun. 'Disembowel Enoch Powell'. *Dissent Magazine* (blog), 2018. www.dissentmagazine.org/online_articles/enoch-powell-racism-neoliberalism-right-wing-populism-rivers-of-blood.

Kundnani, Arun. *The End of Tolerance: Racism in 21st Century Britain*. London: Pluto Press, 2007.

Kundnani, Arun. 'From Oldham to Bradford: The Violence of the Violated'. Institute of Race Relations, 2001. https://irr.org.uk/article/from-oldham-to-bradford-the-violence-of-the-violated/.

The Labour Party Manifesto 2010: A Future Fair for All. London: The Labour Party, 2010.

Laybourn, Keith. 'The Failure of Socialist Unity in Britain c. 1893–1914'. *Transactions of the Royal Historical Society* 4 (1994): 153–75.

Lentin, Alana and Gavan Titley. *The Crises of Multiculturalism: Racism in a Neoliberal Age*. London: Zed Books, 2011.

Lewis, Gail. 'Welcome to the Margins: Diversity, Tolerance, and Policies of Exclusion'. *Ethnic and Racial Studies* 28, no. 3 (2005): 536–58.

Lewis, Gail and Sarah Neal. 'Introduction: Contemporary Political Contexts, Changing Terrains and Revisited Discourses'. *Ethnic and Racial Studies* 28, no. 3 (2005): 423–44.

Lindop, Fred. 'Racism and the Working Class: Strikes in Support of Enoch Powell in 1968'. *Labour History Review* 66, no. 1 (2001): 79–100.

Linebaugh, Peter. *Red Round Globe Hot Burning: A Tale at the Crossroads of Commons and Closure, of Love and Terror, of Race and Class, and of Kate and Ned Despard*. Oakland: University of California Press, 2019.

Little, Allan. 'Scotland's Decision'. BBC, 2014. www.bbc.co.uk/news/special/2014/newsspec_8699/index.html.

Louis, Wm Roger. *The Oxford History of the British Empire: Volume IV: The Twentieth Century*. Edited by Judith Brown and Wm Roger Louis. Oxford: Oxford University Press, 1999.

MacKenzie, John M. and Tom Devine, eds. *Scotland and the British Empire*. Oxford: Oxford University Press, 2016.

Makin-Waite, Mike. *On Burnley Road: Class, Race and Politics in a Northern English Town*. London: Lawrence & Wishart, 2021.

Malik, Kenan. 'How We All Colluded in Fortress Europe'. *The Guardian*, 10 June 2018. www.theguardian.com/commentisfree/2018/jun/10/sunday-essay-how-we-colluded-in-fortress-europe-immigration.

Mandelson, Peter, and Roger Liddle. *The Blair Revolution: Can New Labour Deliver?* London: Faber & Faber, 1996.

Mann, Robin, and Steve Fenton. *Nation, Class and Resentment: The Politics of National Identity in England, Scotland and Wales.* Basingstoke: Palgrave Macmillan, 2017.

Marvin, Jonas. 'Brexit From Below: Nation, Race and Class'. *Salvage* 10 (2021): 53–88.

Marx, Karl. *Capital.* Vol. 1. London: Penguin, 1990.

May, Theresa. 'Statement from the New Prime Minister Theresa May'. Gov.uk, 2016. www.gov.uk/government/speeches/statem ent-from-the-new-prime-minister-theresa-may.

McBriar, Alan M. *Fabian Socialism and English Politics. 1884–1918.* Cambridge: Cambridge University Press, 1963.

McBride, Maureen. 'Nationalism and "Sectarianism" in Contemporary Scotland'. *Ethnic and Racial Studies* 45, no. 16 (2022): 335–58.

McCafferty, Patricia. 'Working the "Third Way": New Labour, Employment Relations and Scottish Devolution'. PhD, University of Glasgow, 2004.

McCartney, Gerry, David Walsh, Lynda Fenton and Rebecca Devine. *Resetting the Course for Population Health: Evidence and Recommendations to Address Stalled Mortality Improvements in Scotland and the Rest of the UK*, May 2022, Glasgow Centre for Population Health, Glasgow, www.gla.ac.uk/media/Media_8526 96_smxx.pdf

McDonnell, Adam and Chris Curtis. 'How Britain Voted in the 2019 General Election'. London: YouGov, 2019. https://yougov.co.uk/ topics/politics/articles-reports/2019/12/17/how-britain-voted-2019-general-election.

McGeever, Brendan and Satnam Virdee. 'Antisemitism and Socialist Strategy in Europe, 1880–1917: An Introduction'. *Patterns of Prejudice* 51, no. 3–4 (2017): 221–34.

McIlroy, John. *Trade Unions in Britain Today.* Second Edition. Manchester: Manchester University Press, 1995.

McIlvanney, William. *Surviving the Shipwreck.* Edinburgh: Mainstream Publishing, 1991.

McVeigh, Robbie. 'Living the Peace Process in Reverse: Racist Violence and British Nationalism in Northern Ireland'. *Race & Class* 56, no. 4 (2015): 3–25.

Meer, Nasar. *The Cruel Optimism of Racial Justice.* Bristol: Policy Press, 2022.

Meer, Nasar. 'Looking up in Scotland? Multinationalism, Multiculturalism and Political Elites'. *Ethnic and Racial Studies* 38, no. 9 (2015): 1477–96.

Meghji, Ali. 'Towards a Theoretical Synergy: Critical Race Theory and Decolonial Thought in Trumpamerica and Brexit Britain'. *Current Sociology* 70, no. 2 (2020): 647–64.

Meth, Monty. *Brothers to All Men? Report on Trade Union Actions and Attitudes on Race Relations*. London: The Runnymede Trust, 1972.

Middleton, Alex. 'The Second Reform Act and the Politics of Empire'. *Parliamentary History* 36, no. 1 (2017): 82–96.

Miles, Robert and Diana Kay. 'The TUC, Foreign Labour and the Labour Government, 1945–1951'. *Immigrants & Minorities* 9, no. 1 (1990): 85–108.

Miliband, David, ed. *Reinventing the Left*. Cambridge: Polity Press, 1994.

Miliband, Ralph. *Parliamentary Socialism: A Study in the Politics of Labour*. London: Merlin Press, 1987.

Modood, Tariq. 'Ethnic Difference and Racial Equality: New Challenges for the Left'. In *Reinventing the Left*, edited by David Miliband. Cambridge: Polity Press, 1994.

Mondon, Aurelien, and Aaron Winter. *Reactionary Democracy: How Racism and the Populist Far Right Became Mainstream*. London: Verso Books, 2020.

Moran, Michael. *The Politics of Industrial Relations*. London: Palgrave Macmillan, 1980.

Morgan, Kevin, Gidon Cohen, and Andrew Flinn. *Communists and British Society 1920–1991: People of a Special Mould*. London: Rivers Oram Press, 2005.

Muggeridge, Anna. 'The Missing Two Million: The Exclusion of Working-Class Women from the 1918 Representation of the People Act'. *Revue Française de Civilisation Britannique. French Journal of British Studies* 23, no. 1 (2018): xxiii–1.

Mullen, Stephen. 'Ae Fond Kiss, and Then We Sever!' *Variant* 35 (2009): 8–10.

Mullen, Stephen. 'Centring Transatlantic Slavery in Scottish Historiography'. *History Compass* 20, no. 1 (2022).

Mullen, Stephen. *The Glasgow Sugar Aristocracy: Scotland and Caribbean Slavery*. London: University of London Press, 2022.

Mullen, Stephen. 'Henry Dundas: A "Great Delayer" of the Abolition

of the Transatlantic Slave Trade'. *The Scottish Historical Review*
100, no. 2 (2021): 218–48.

Mullen, Stephen. *It Wisnae Us: The Truth About Glasgow and
Slavery*. Edinburgh: The Royal Incorporation of Architects in
Scotland, 2009.

Mullen, Stephen and Gibbs, Ewan. 'Scotland, Atlantic Slavery and
the Scottish National Party: From colonised to coloniser in the
political imagination'. *Nations and Nationalism* (2023): 1–17.

Museum Galleries Scotland. 'Empire, Slavery & Scotland's
Museums', 2021. www.museumsgalleriesscotland.org.uk/proje
cts/empire-slavery-scotlands-museums/.

Nairn, Tom. *The Break-Up of Britain: Crisis and Neo-Nationalism*.
Third Edition. London: Verso Books, 2021.

Nairn, Tom. 'The English Working Class'. *New Left Review* 1, no.
24 (1964): 43–57.

Nairn, Tom. 'Enoch Powell: The New Right'. *New Left Review* 1,
no. 61 (1970): 3–27.

Nairn, Tom. 'Labour Imperialism'. *New Left Review* 1, no. 32
(1965): 3–15.

Nairn, Tom. 'The Nature of the Labour Party (Part II)'. *New Left
Review* 1, no. 28 (1964): 33–62.

Nairn, Tom. 'Union on the Rocks?' *New Left Review* 1, no. 42
(2007): 117–32.

Narayan, John. 'The Wages of Whiteness in the Absence of
Wages: Racial Capitalism, Reactionary Intercommunalism and
the Rise of Trumpism'. *Third World Quarterly* 38, no. 11
(2017): 2482–500.

National Audit Office. 'Taxpayer Support for UK Banks: FAQs –
National Audit Office (NAO)', 2020. www.nao.org.uk/high
lights/taxpayer-support-for-uk-banks-faqs/.

National Centre for Social Research. *1982, British Social Attitudes
Survey*. London: National Centre for Social Research, 1982.

Noronha, Luke de. *Deporting Black Britons: Portraits of Deportation
to Jamaica*. Manchester: Manchester University Press, 2020.

Obolenskaya, Polina, and John Hills. 'Flat-Lining or Seething
beneath the Surface? Two Decades of Changing Economic
Inequality in the UK'. *Oxford Review of Economic Policy* 35,
no. 3 (2019): 467–89.

Owen, David. 'Ethnic Minorities in Great Britain: Patterns of
Population Change, 1981–91'. Census Statistical Paper.

Coventry: Centre for Research in Ethnic Relations, University of Warwick, 1995.

Panitch, Leo and Colin Leys. *Searching for Socialism: The Project of the Labour New Left from Benn to Corbyn*. London: Verso Books, 2020.

Parekh, Bhikhu. *The Future of Multi-Ethnic Britain. The Parekh Report*. London: Profile Books Ltd, 2000.

Parekh, Bhikhu. 'Minority Rights, Majority Values'. In *Reinventing the Left*, edited by David Miliband. Cambridge: Polity Press, 1994.

Parmar, Pratibha. 'Black Feminism: The Politics of Articulation'. In *Identity: Community, Culture, Difference*, edited by Jonathan Rutherford, 101–26. London: Lawrence & Wishart, 1990.

Partington, Richard. 'Labour to Pledge "Ironclad Discipline" with Public Finances'. *The Guardian*, 12 July 2022.

Patel, Ian Sanjay. *We're Here Because You Were There: Immigration and the End of Empire*. London: Verso Books, 2021.

Paton, Kirsteen. *Gentrification: A Working-Class Perspective*. London: Routledge, 2014.

Paul, Kathleen. *Whitewashing Britain: Race and Citizenship in the Postwar Era*. Ithaca, NY: Cornell University Press, 1997.

Peplow, Simon. *Race and Riots in Thatcher's Britain*. Manchester: Manchester University Press, 2019.

Phillips, Kate. *Bought & Sold: Scotland, Jamaica and Slavery*. Edinburgh: Luath Press, 2022.

Piacentini, Teresa, Smina Akhtar, Gareth Mulvey and Ashli Mullen. '"It's Not like It Just Happened That Day": Anti-Racist Solidarity in Two Glasgow Neighbourhoods'. In *Social Movements and Everyday Acts of Resistance: Solidarity in a Changing World*, edited by Stamatis Poulakidakos, Anastasia Veneti and Maria Rovisco. New York: Routledge, 2022.

Pitcher, Ben. *The Politics of Multiculturalism: Race and Racism in Contemporary Britain*. Basingstoke: Palgrave Macmillan, 2009.

Poulantzas, Nicos. *State, Power, Socialism*. London: NLB, 1978.

Ramamurthy, Anandi. *Black Star: Britain's Asian Youth Movements*. London: Pluto Press, 2013.

Renshaw, Daniel. *Socialism and the Diasporic 'Other': A Comparative Study of Irish Catholic and Jewish Radical and Communal Politics in East London, 1889–1912*. Liverpool: Liverpool University Press, 2018.

Renton, David. *When We Touched the Sky: The Anti-Nazi League 1977–1981*. London: New Clarion Press, 2006.

Reyes, Oscar. 'New Labour's Politics of the Hard-Working Family'. In *Discourse Theory in European Politics: Identity, Policy and Governance*, edited by David Howarth and Jacob Torfing, 231–54. London: Palgrave Macmillan, 2005. DOI: 10.1057/9780230523364_10.

'The "Riots"'. *Race & Class* 23, no. 2–3 (1981): 223–32.

Roberts, Matthew. 'Resisting "Arithmocracy": Parliament, Community, and the Third Reform Act'. *Journal of British Studies* 50, no. 2 (2011): 381–409.

Rogaly, Ben. *Stories from a Migrant City: Living and Working Together in the Shadow of Brexit*. Manchester: Manchester University Press, 2020.

Rose, Jonathan. *The Intellectual Life of the British Working Classes*. New Haven: Yale University Press, 2002.

Roth, Andrew. *Enoch Powell: Tory Tribune*. London: TBS The Book Service Ltd, 1970.

Runnymede Trust. 'Bulletin: Runnymede's Quarterly'. London: Runnymede Trust, December 2000.

Saunders, Robert. 'The Politics of Reform and the Making of the Second Reform Act, 1848–1867'. *The Historical Journal* 50, no. 3 (2007): 571–91.

Saville, John. *1848: The British State and the Chartist Movement*. Cambridge: Cambridge University Press, 1987.

Schofield, Camilla. *Enoch Powell and the Making of Postcolonial Britain*. Cambridge: Cambridge University Press, 2013.

Schwartz, Laura. *Feminism and the Servant Problem: Class and Domestic Labour in the Women's Suffrage Movement*. Cambridge: Cambridge University Press, 2019.

Schwarz, Bill. '"The Only White Man in There": The Re-Racialisation of England, 1956–1968'. *Race & Class* 38, no. 1 (1996): 65–78.

'Scottish Social Attitudes 2015: Attitudes to Discrimination and Positive Action'. Scottish Government, 2016. www.gov.scot/publications/scottish-social-attitudes-2015-attitudes-discrimination-positive-action/.

Seymour, Richard. *Corbyn: The Strange Rebirth of Radical Politics*. London: Verso Books, 2016.

Shaw, Eric. *Losing Labour's Soul? New Labour and the Blair Government 1997–2007*. London: Routledge, 2008.

Shaw, Martin. *Political Racism: Brexit and Its Aftermath*. Newcastle upon Tyne: Agenda Publishing, 2022.

Sherwood, Marika. *Claudia Jones: A Life in Exile*. First Edition. London: Lawrence & Wishart, 1999.

Shilliam, Robbie. 'Enoch Powell: Britain's First Neoliberal Politician'. *New Political Economy* 26, no. 2 (2021): 239–49.

Shilliam, Robbie. *Race and the Undeserving Poor: From Abolition to Brexit*. Newcastle upon Tyne: Agenda Publishing, 2018.

Shukra, Kalbir. 'A Scramble for the British Pie'. *Patterns of Prejudice* 30, no. 1 (1996): 28–36.

Sivanandan, Ambalavaner. *Communities of Resistance: Writings on Black Struggles for Socialism*. London: Verso Books, 1990.

Sivanandan, Ambalavaner. *A Different Hunger: Writings on Black Resistance*. London: Pluto Press, 1982.

Smith, Evan. '"Class before Race": British Communism and the Place of Empire in Postwar Race Relations'. *Science & Society* 72, no. 4 (2008): 455–81.

Solomos, John. *Race and Racism in Britain*. Third Edition. Basingstoke: Palgrave Macmillan, 2003.

Streeck, Wolfgang. 'The Crises of Democratic Capitalism'. *New Left Review* 1, no. 71 (2011): 5–29.

Sturge, Georgina. 'General Election 2019: Brexit'. House of Commons Library, 2020. https://commonslibrary.parliament.uk/general-election-2019-brexit/.

Sundari, Anitha and Ruth Pearson. *Striking Women: Struggles & Strategies of South Asian Women Workers from Grunwick to Gate Gourmet*. Chadwell Heath: Lawrence & Wishart, 2018.

Sutcliffe-Braithwaite, Florence. *Class, Politics, and the Decline of Deference in England, 1968–2000*. Oxford: Oxford University Press, 2018.

Sveinsson, Kjartan Páll. *Who Cares about the White Working Class?* London: Runnymede Trust, 2009.

Thompson, Edward Palmer. *The Making of the English Working Class*. London: Penguin, 1991.

Tilly, Charles. 'Democratization: Working Paper'. *Institute of Governmental Studies* 98, no. 7 (1998): 1–13.

Travis, Alan. 'After 44 Years Secret Papers Reveal Truth about Five Nights of Violence in Notting Hill'. *The Guardian*, 24 August 2002. www.theguardian.com/uk/2002/aug/24/artsandhumanities.nottinghillcarnival2002.

Travis, Alan. 'Blunkett Remedy for Anti-Social Behaviour'. *The Guardian*, 30 January 2002. www.theguardian.com/politics/2002/jan/30/ukcrime.immigrationpolicy.

'The True Cost of Austerity and Inequality – UK Case Study'. Oxfam International, 2013. www-cdn.oxfam.org/s3fs-public/file_atta chments/cs-true-cost-austerity-inequality-uk-120913-en_0.pdf.

Tyler, Gloria. 'Food Banks in the UK'. London: House of Commons Library, 2021. https://commonslibrary.parliament.uk/research-briefings/cbp-8585/.

Tyler, Imogen. *Revolting Subjects*. London: Zed Books, 2013.

UNISON The Public Service Union. 'Cuts to Local Services', 2014. www.unison.org.uk/at-work/local-government/key-issues/cuts-to-local-services/.

University of Glasgow. 'Historical Slavery Initiative', 2021. www.gla.ac.uk/explore/historicalslaveryinitiative/.

Valluvan, Sivamohan. *The Clamour of Nationalism: Race and Nation in Twenty-First-Century Britain*. Manchester: Manchester University Press, 2019.

Valluvan, Sivamohan. 'Conviviality and Multiculture: A Post-Integration Sociology of Multi-Ethnic Interaction'. *YOUNG* 24, no. 3 (2016): 204–21.

Vellacott, Jo. *Pacifists, Patriots and the Vote: The Erosion of Democratic Suffragism in Britain During the First World War*. New York: Palgrave Macmillan, 2007.

Verberckmoes, Johan. 'The United Kingdom: Between Policy and Practice'. In *The Lost Perspective? Trade Unions between Ideology and Social Action in the New Europe*, edited by Patrick Pasture, Johan Verberckmoes and Hans de Witte. Aldershot: Avebury, 1996.

Vernon, James. 'The History of Britain Is Dead; Long Live a Global History of Britain'. *History Australia* 13, no. 1 (2016): 19–34.

Virdee, Satnam. 'Class, Racism and the Politics of Vacuum'. In *Corbynism from Below*, edited by Mark Perryman, 208–19. London: Lawrence & Wishart, 2019.

Virdee, Satnam. 'The Lines of Descent of the Present Crisis'. *Sociological Review* 71, no. 2 (2023).

Virdee, Satnam. '"Race", Employment and Social Change: A Critique of Current Orthodoxies'. *Ethnic and Racial Studies* 29, no. 4 (2006): 605–28.

Virdee, Satnam. *Racism, Class and the Racialized Outsider*. London: Palgrave Macmillan, 2014.

Virdee, Satnam, Christopher Kyriakides and Tariq Modood. 'Codes of Cultural Belonging: Racialised National Identities in a Multi-Ethnic Scottish Neighbourhood'. *Sociological Research Online* 11, no. 4 (2006). www.socresonline.org.uk/11/4/virdee. html.

Vize, Richard. 'Public Sector Workers Have Been Pummelled by Austerity. It's a Scandal'. *The Guardian*, 1 October 2018. www. theguardian.com/society/2018/oct/01/public-sector-workers-pummelled-austerity-scandal.

Ware, Vron. 'Towards a Sociology of Resentment: A Debate on Class and Whiteness'. *Sociological Research Online* 13, no. 5 (2008). www.socresonline.org.uk/13/5/9.html.bak.

Waters, Rob. *Thinking Black: Britain, 1964–1985*. Berkeley: University of California Press, 2018.

Watkins, Johnathan, Wahyu Wulaningsih, Charlie Da Zhou, Dominic C. Marshall, Guia D. C. Sylianteng, Phyllis G. Dela Rosa, Viveka A. Miguel, Rosalind Raine, Lawrence P. King and Mahiben Maruthappu. 'Effects of Health and Social Care Spending Constraints on Mortality in England: A Time Trend Analysis'. *BMJ Open* 7, no. 11 (2017): e017722. DOI: 10.1136/bmjopen-2017-017722.

Watkins, Susan. 'Britain's Decade of Crisis'. *New Left Review* 1, no. 121 (2020): 5–19.

'What Does The 2011 Census Tell Us About Inter-Ethnic Relationships?' 2011 Census Analysis. London: Office for National Statistics, 2011. www.ons.gov.uk/peoplepopulationandcommun ity/birthsdeathsandmarriages/marriagecohabitationandcivilp artnerships/articles/whatdoesthe2011censustellusaboutinter ethnicrelationships/2014-07-03.

Widgery, David. *Beating Time: Riot 'n' Race 'n' Rock 'n' Roll*. London: Chatto & Windus, 1986.

Widgery, David. *The Left in Britain 1956–1968*. London: Penguin, 1976.

William, Eichler. 'Around 25% of Local Government Jobs "Slashed" Due to Austerity'. *LocalGov.Co.Uk* (blog), 2019. www.local gov.co.uk/Around-25-of-local-government-jobs-slashed-due-to-austerity/47647.

Williams, Eric. *Capitalism and Slavery*. London: Deutsch, 1964.

Williams, Raymond. *Resources of Hope: Culture, Democracy, Socialism*. London: Verso Books, 1989.

Wintour, Patrick. 'Anger after Harriet Harman Says Labour Will Not Vote against Welfare Bill'. *The Guardian*, 12 July 2015. www.theguardian.com/politics/2015/jul/12/harman-labour-not-vote-against-welfare-bill-limit-child-tax-credits.

Wintour, Patrick and Vikram Dodd. 'Blair Blames Spate of Murders on Black Culture'. *The Guardian*, 12 April 2007. www.theguardian.com/politics/2007/apr/12/ukcrime.race.

Wright, Oliver and Jerome Taylor. 'Cameron: My War on Multiculturalism'. *The Independent*, 5 February 2011. www.independent.co.uk/news/uk/politics/cameron-my-war-on-multiculturalism-2205074.html.

Wyn Jones, Richard, Guy Lodge, Ailsa Henderson and Daniel Wincott. 'The Dog That Finally Barked: England as an Emerging Political Community'. London: Institute for Public Policy Research, 2012. www.ippr.org/research/publications/the-dog-that-finally-barked-england-as-an-emerging-political-community.

'Young Fathers Suffer Backlash over Art Galleries Criticism', 2017. www.scotsman.com/arts-and-culture/young-fathers-suffer-backlash-over-art-galleries-criticism-1443792.

Young, James D. *The Rousing of the Scottish Working Class 1774–2008*. Glasgow: Clydeside Press, 2009.

Young, Robert C. *The Idea of English Ethnicity*. Oxford: Blackwell Publishing, 2007.

Younge, Gary. 'Britain Is Again White'. *The Guardian*, 18 February 2002. www.theguardian.com/world/2002/feb/18/race.politics.

Index

Printed in the USA
CPSIA information can be obtained
at www.ICGtesting.com
LVHW041153101023
PP17922000018B/167

9 781526 164599